UNSHAKEABLE
TRUST

UNSHAKEABLE
TRUST

Find the Joy of Trusting God at All Times,
in All Things

JOYCE MEYER

Faith
Words

NEW YORK NASHVILLE

FaithWords
Hachette Book Group
1290 Avenue of the Americas, New York, NY 10104
faithwords.com
twitter.com/faithwords

First published in hardcover and ebook in September 2017
First U.S. Trade Paperback Edition: October 2018

FaithWords is a division of Hachette Book Group, Inc. The FaithWords name and
logo are trademarks of Hachette Book Group, Inc.

The publisher is not responsible for websites (or their content)
that are not owned by the publisher.

The Hachette Speakers Bureau provides a wide range of authors for speaking events.
To find out more, go to www.hachettespeakersbureau.com or call (866) 376-6591.

ISBNs: 978-1-4555-6009-7 (trade paperback), 978-1-4555-6005-9 (ebook)

Printed in the United States of America

LSC-C

Printing 4, 2020

CONTENTS

I cannot think of any subject that is more important to write about than trusting God. It is a vital subject because once we choose to trust God, the benefits are countless and amazing. Trusting God is one of the greatest ways to honor Him.

From the very beginning of this book, I want to emphasize that trust is not an obligation that we owe God; it is a privilege that He makes available to us. We are invited to trust God, and by doing so, we open the door to a life of peace, joy, and fruitfulness.

When we mix a healthy portion of trusting God into everything that we do, it enables us to live without worry, anxiety, fear, reasoning, or debilitating stress. For example, I am trusting God to help me write this book. That means I recognize that I don't know everything I need to know about trusting Him and am convinced that without Him, the book will not be good. God wants us to lean on Him at all times and in all things. Nothing is too small for God to be involved in where His children are concerned.

Since individuals tend to be self-reliant and independent, it usually takes us quite a while to learn how to trust God. Part of the difficulty stems from our unpleasant experiences that often teach us that people cannot always be trusted. But God's ways are far above those of people, and His Word teaches us that His character is such that He cannot lie or deceive.

In this book, I hope to share with you that you can learn to *trust without borders* and have *faith beyond reason*. Total trust in

God should be our goal, not only because it honors God, but also because the benefits are astounding.

When we trust God, it pleases Him. Hebrews 11:6 says that "without faith it is impossible to please Him" (NKJV). Faith and trust are so connected that we cannot separate them. Faith is the substance that invites God into our lives. It maintains His presence in our lives and connects us to Him in a very powerful way.

We have an enemy, Satan, who continually seeks to prevent us from enjoying relationship with God and the life He offers us. Satan tempts us with fear, worry and anxiety, reasoning, stress, doubt, and many other things that take our mind off God and cause us to lead self-absorbed lives in which we desperately try to take care of ourselves.

The only antidote for these miseries is complete trust in God. I pray that as you read this book, you will receive grace to completely release yourself and all that concerns you to God, in every situation and at all times.

As you read and study this book, keep this Scripture in mind:

> [Most] blessed is the man who believes in, trusts in, and relies on the Lord, and whose hope and confidence the Lord is.
>
> Jeremiah 17:7 (AMPC)

UNSHAKEABLE
TRUST

CHAPTER 1

What Is Trust?

The beginning of anxiety is the end of faith, and the beginning of faith is the end of anxiety.

George Mueller

Anytime we trust anyone or anything that proves trustworthy, it puts an end to anxiety. Therefore it is very important to learn what trust is and how to trust. We especially want to learn to trust God.

Noah Webster's 1828 dictionary defines trust as: "Confidence; a reliance or resting of the mind on the integrity, veracity, justice, friendship or other sound principle of another person."[1] He who puts his trust in the Lord will be safe (see Proverbs 29:25).

Trust enables us to live without weights, burdens, or cares because we have confidence that another will deal with those things for us. Instead of feeling that we are con-

> Trust enables us to live without weights, burdens, or cares.

tinually carrying a heavy load, we can enjoy a wonderful lightness in our souls.

Putting our trust in God and casting our cares on Him requires that we make a decision to do it. The psalmist David spoke frequently about putting his trust in God. The word "put" is an action word that we often find in God's Word when He is giving us instructions on what to do—things like *put on love, put on the new man, put on your shoes of peace,* as well as *put your trust in God.* (See Colossians 3:14; Ephesians 4:24; Ephesians 6:15; Proverbs 3:5.)

The Bible says, "Cast your burden on the Lord [releasing the weight of it] and He will sustain you..." (Psalm 55:22 [AMPC]). I like the idea of releasing the weight of a burden. We often live with a heavy heart and a burdened mind, but God is inviting us to a better quality of life that is only experienced by putting our trust in Him. Noah Webster said that trust is a resting of the mind. The apostle Paul confirmed this when he said that those who believe (trust) God will enter His rest (see Hebrews 4:3).

One of the ways we can discern that we are truly trusting God, rather than merely trying to trust Him, is whether or not our souls are resting in God's faithfulness. If I say I am trusting God, but I continue to carry the weight of the burden by worrying and being anxious, then I have not released the burden to the Lord. I may want to. I may be trying to. But I have not done it yet.

Understanding this has helped me to learn what real trust in God is. It is more than words—it is releasing the weight of my burden; a decisive action that brings rest to my soul (mind, will, emotions). Just imagine that you are carrying a backpack filled with rocks everywhere you go. You take it to work, to the market, to church, and it is a heavy burden, but you continue to carry it. Now imagine that you decide to drop it—just think how much better you would feel and how much easier everything would be.

That's the way it is when we worry and carry the weight of burdens with us instead of entrusting them to God. We continue functioning

> *You can decide to drop your burden today.*

and doing what we need to do, but the weight of the burden places a great deal of stress on us and makes our life very difficult. You can decide to drop your burden today by trusting God, if you choose to, and you will be glad you did.

I encounter many people who are quick to tell me that they are trusting God to take care of their problems, and yet, they also tell me they are afraid, worried, and desperately trying to reason out what they should do. This tells me they believe they should trust God, and they want to trust God, but they haven't done so yet. They say they trust God, yet they are weighed down with the cares of many things.

I've learned that the best way to function in our relationship with God is to be truthful with Him. He already knows the truth, but it will help us to face it. I wasted a lot of years claiming that I was trusting God while I was worried and miserable, and it really helped me to recognize that true trust has good fruit. It produces peace—the peace that passes understanding!

If a person has not yet come to the point of being able to trust God totally, it is best to be honest with God about it. In Mark chapter 9, there is a good story about a father who sought healing for his son. He told Jesus that he believed but needed help with his unbelief (see Mark 9:24). I have always liked his honesty, and the good news is that he received his miracle. We all have some doubt mixed in with our faith at times. Hopefully, we are growing and learning to trust God more all the time, but growth takes time and there is no reason to be condemned if your trust in God is not perfected yet.

I have been teaching God's Word for over forty years, and yet I have learned a lot about trusting God in the past year. I strongly imagine that I will learn even more while I am studying and doing research for this book.

The Character of God

The Merriam-Webster.com dictionary defines trust as: "belief that someone or something is reliable, good, honest, effective, etc."[2] Trust is dependent on what we know about the character of the one being trusted. If we cannot believe the person is good, just, kind, loving, and trustworthy, then we cannot put our confidence in them.

I have found that a thorough study on the character of God has helped me tremendously in learning how to put my complete trust in God. For example, one of the aspects of God's character that gives me a lot of comfort is that He is just. That means that He will always make wrong things right.

I have experienced His justice in my life many times, and when I am enduring what seems to me to be unjust or unfair treatment, I can trust God to make the wrong thing right in His own way and timing. Life is not always fair, but God is, and when we put our trust in Him, releasing the weight of our burden, He works in our behalf and brings justice in our situation.

Trusting God to bring justice relieves me of the job of trying to do it myself. God says clearly in His Word that vengeance is His and that He repays the enemies of His people:

> For we know Him who said, "Vengeance is Mine [retribution and the deliverance of justice rest with Me], I will repay [the wrongdoer]." And again, "The Lord will judge His people."
>
> Hebrews 10:30

In order to experience the justice of God, we must be willing to turn the situation over to Him and refuse to try and take care of it ourselves. This is the hard part! For me, and I think for most of us, we usually wear ourselves out trying to take care of ourselves, unsuccessfully, until we finally are willing to give trusting God a try. Once we do that and begin to experience His faithfulness, it becomes easier to trust again and again. One of the reasons why trusting God can be challenging is because He doesn't always immediately give us what we ask for. We receive from God through faith and patience. The waiting part is a test that usually stretches our faith to new levels.

God is good, merciful, holy, and kind. He is gracious and He is faithful and true. God is love! He is the same at all times, and we can depend on Him to keep His word.

It is easy to put our trust in someone we believe loves us and not only has the power to help us, but also wants to help us! God is waiting to help you and me, and all we need to do is trust Him to do so.

As I look back over my life, I can definitely say that God is faithful. He is always there for us, even when we don't see Him or feel Him. As long as we believe He is working, He will manifest, or reveal, the evidence of His work at the right time. Don't give up when the wait seems long; continue trusting God!

Anytime I am having difficulty trusting God, I remember things He has done for me in the past and I am reassured that He will do it again. I have kept journals for forty years, and I ran across one recently from the 1970s, when I asked God to provide me with a dozen new dishtowels. Dave and I had no money to purchase them, and since I was just beginning my journey of trusting God, I approached Him as a little child and asked for them. Imagine my elation when a few weeks later, a woman I was barely acquainted with showed up at my door and said, "I hope you don't think I'm crazy, but I kept feeling that God wanted me to bring you some new dishtowels!" I got so excited that she was shocked until I explained to her that I had asked God to provide them. That is one of my vivid experiences with the faithfulness of God, and there have been many others through the years.

In the Bible, we read that when David needed to kill the giant, Goliath, and everyone was discouraging him and telling him that he would fail, he remembered the lion and the bear that he had previously killed with God's faithful help. His faith was strengthened and he went on to slay Goliath. (See 1 Samuel 17:34–36.)

I want to encourage you to take time, perhaps even right now, to make a list of some of the times you have experienced God's faithfulness in your own life. I can assure you that it will feed your faith and enable you to trust God more easily for the current needs in your life.

I have heard the word "faithful" defined as "to be trusted or relied on." We can rely on God! We can lean on Him. He has promised to never leave us or forsake us, but to be with us always (see Matthew 28:20).

When we are in need, we can trust Him to be with us and help us (see Hebrews 13:5). When we are going through trials, He is with us and always helps us (see 1 Corinthians 10:13). And when all others forsake us, He is with us and remains faithful (see 2 Timothy 4:16–17).

A sincere study of each aspect of God's character is very beneficial in helping us learn to trust Him. I will mention more of His character traits throughout the book, but I also encourage you to seek out resources on this subject and do your own study.

Confidence

Trust is said to be confidence! We all know how much easier life is when we have confidence. Having a belief that we can do a thing enables us to live life boldly with joy and positive expectation. As believers in Jesus, our confidence needs to be in Him. We all have confidence in some areas, but we can be confident in all areas of life through trusting God. For example, sometimes I feel confident when I am teaching in a conference, but there are also times when I don't. In those times I can choose to be confident as long as my confidence is in Christ and not in myself or how I feel.

The apostle Paul was very clear when he stated that he put no confidence in the flesh. Although he had many natural advantages, he did not put his trust in those outward things. He emphatically says that our confidence is in Christ (see Philippians 3:3). Trust is confidence in the one who is trusted, and confidence in Christ makes us comfortable! It allows us to work with ease

> Trust is confidence in the one who is trusted.

because we believe we can do what needs to be done. Confident trust removes stress, pressure, worry, and the fear of failure.

I said that we can "be" confident even when we don't "feel" confident, and this is a very important point. Feelings are fickle; they are likely to change at any time and without notice, so putting our confidence in how we feel isn't very smart.

You might go to apply for a job and initially feel confident because you believe you have the skills needed. But halfway through your interview, you get the feeling that the person interviewing you doesn't like you very much, and suddenly that thought (which may not even be true) causes you to lose your feeling of confidence. However, if your confidence is in God, you can trust Him to give you favor, and you can continue the interview while being confident that if it is the right job for you, you will get it.

Satan does not want us to be confident because he knows that without it, we will not accomplish much in life. Even people who are very talented, intelligent, and capable still need confidence.

Confidence is to us what fuel is to an airplane: An airplane has the capability to fly, yet it remains on the ground without fuel.

It is impossible to be consistently confident if our confidence is misplaced in people or things, because they are changeable, but God never changes and He does not lie! He is the Rock we hang on to in a world that is often a swirling sea of uncertainty.

CHAPTER 2

Trust Brings Rest

Come to Me, all you who labor and are heavy-laden and overburdened, and I will cause you to rest...

Matthew 11:28 (AMPC)

In Noah Webster's definition of trust, he indicates that it is a resting of the mind on the good character of someone else. I feel it is important to dedicate a chapter in this book to the thought of resting the mind. This is something we all desperately need and most of us want. There are far too many things in our lives that need attention for us to be able to think about all of them without feeling overwhelmed. God wants to help us, but as long as we continue trying to do it all ourselves, He won't force His help on us.

God often offers us help by providing other people to help share our load in life. Dave and I have two sons who work with us in the ministry, and God has provided them to help us by sharing the load of managing a large ministry. It was difficult at first for us to let go of things we had previously been in charge of and to commit those things to our sons. It was a decision we had to make, and doing so has given us great rest of mind and soul.

There are many things and situations that we no longer have to think about because our sons take care of them for us. I am free to teach, write, pray, study, and do my television show. As I sit here and write, there are many things going on at the ministry that I am not even aware of. I see the result and it is always good, but I trust my sons to manage all the aspects of getting us to that result. My son Dan just told me yesterday that our television program is now on Netflix, and I was pleasantly surprised. That is a great opportunity to reach more people, and it all happened without me being involved because I released that part of the management of the ministry to someone else.

My son David surprised me when he showed me pictures of a project in Tanzania that we are funding and overseeing. I get the joy of sharing in the celebration of helping more people, but I didn't have to worry even one time about any of the thousands of details that went into making the project a success.

Our sons are partnering with us in the ministry, and although we still work hard, we are not overburdened and overloaded. We are not pressed down with worry and concern. Our minds are at rest!

God delights in surprising us and will often do so if we will put things into His hands and safekeeping. He wants to partner with us in our lives, and when we let Him do so, our minds can be at rest. According to Scripture, we are called into companionship and participation with God. 1 Corinthians 1:9 (AMPC) says it this way:

> God is faithful (reliable, trustworthy, and therefore ever true to His promise, and He can be depended on); by Him you were called into companionship and participation with His Son, Jesus Christ our Lord.

A relationship with God is much more than reading Scripture each day, going to church once a week, giving some money in the offering, and perhaps doing a few good deeds. That is mere religion, but the rich and wonderful relationship we are offered through faith in Christ is a partnership. He gives us ability and expects us to use it, all the while trusting in Him. He is also ready to handle anything we cannot handle. I like to say, *Trust God to help you do your best, and trust Him to do the rest.*

> *Trust God to help you do your best, and trust Him to do the rest.*

Peace of Mind

God offers us peace of mind when we place our trust in Him. Throughout each day, many thoughts come to mind that can cause worry and concern. This morning I was with someone who was very quiet and not interested in having any conversation with me, and my thoughts went something like this: *I don't think she likes me very much.* As I thought that, I started feeling that perhaps I needed to "do something" to change the situation, and yet I did not have any idea what I could do.

When we try to do things that we have no idea how to do, it always creates stress, concern, worry, and sometimes fear. Are there things in your life that you feel responsible to "fix" but you have no idea what to do about them? If so, you can do what I did this morning and pray, committing the situation to God and trusting Him to "fix it." I prayed a simple prayer and said, "Father, I put my relationship with _____ into Your hands. I commit it to You and ask You to make it what You want it to be." As soon as I did that, my peace of mind returned.

Shortly after that, I heard from one of my children and I could tell they were not doing well emotionally. I asked if I could help in any way, but they said no, and immediately my thought was, *I wonder what's wrong? Did they argue with someone? Do they feel bad physically? What happened?* I had my backpack loaded up and was ready to carry it all day when I remembered that I could release it to God, who was the only one who knew what was wrong and what to do about it.

I prayed, "Father, help _____ decide to have a good day. Let them see how blessed they are and be thankful instead of sad." Shortly after that prayer I received this text: "I feel much better now. I love you!"

We may experience many things like this each day. It is no wonder that people are stressed-out unless they know how to trust God and cast their cares on Him. I was one of those people for over half of my life, but I am very grateful to now know what to do with my cares.

Let God share your day by talking with Him about everything. Prayer is simply talking with God, so I urge you not to see it as a duty we need to perform. Prayer is our way of letting God into every aspect of our lives, including the ones that attempt to steal our peace and cause us anxiety.

Don't be deceived into believing that you have no choice in what you think about. If the thoughts in your mind are worried or anxious, you can choose to think about something else. God's Word teaches us to cast down wrong thoughts, bringing all of them into captivity to the obedience of Christ (see 2 Corinthians 10:5). I find that talking to Jesus all throughout the day, about all that I do, and any concern I have is one of the best ways to stay in fellowship with Him, enjoy His presence, and at the same time receive help from Him.

What would Jesus think when He had a situation that would be classified as a "trouble"? We have many examples in the Bible of how He handled such situations, and in each case, He made the choice to trust His Father in Heaven. Even when He was on the cross and felt that He had been abandoned, He said, "Father, into Your hands I commit My spirit!" (Luke 23:46 [AMPC]). This was the most difficult time of His life and yet, in the midst of terrible pain and suffering, He trusted God!

The Bible also gives us an account of Jesus being in a boat when a huge storm of hurricane proportions arose. The disciples who were with Him became frantic, timid and fearful, but He was in the stern of the boat asleep. When they woke Him up and expressed their fear, Jesus said, "Why are you so timid and fearful? How is it that you have no faith (no firmly relying trust)?" (Mark 4:40 [AMPC]).

God expects us to trust Him! He offers us that option, and we would all be wise if we learn to choose it anytime we are tempted to worry. Why be miserable when we don't have to be?

What If I Don't Get What I Want?

I think the fear of not getting what we want is a root cause of the difficulty we have in learning how to trust God. Most of us are convinced that the only way we can be assured of getting what we want is if we take care of ourselves. This fear prevents us from completely trusting anyone.

Because I was raised by a selfish and abusive father and mother, I felt certain that nobody truly had my best interests in mind. My attitude was, *If I don't take care of myself, nobody will!* Perhaps you recognize that attitude and it has made you as miserable as it did me.

Dave was often hurt by my unwillingness to trust him, but I was not convinced that he would not make selfish decisions that only benefited him. I believed that he loved me, but my parents had also told me that they loved me, and I saw how that turned out. I

> God always has our best interest in His thoughts and plans for us.

could not learn to trust anyone until I came to believe in the unconditional love of God and realized that even if a person did hurt me, God would heal and comfort me. God always has our best interest in His thoughts and plans for us, and once we believe that, we can trust Him and learn to trust others.

Trusting God doesn't guarantee that we will always get what we want. However, if we don't, it is only because God has something better in mind for us. Many times in my life, I wanted and asked God for things that I didn't get, only to realize later that if God had given me what I wanted at the time, it would not have been good for me. As we learn to want what God wants for us even more than what we ourselves want, we can have peace of mind in every situation.

Jesus gave us a perfect example of this type of attitude when He prayed in the Garden of Gethsemane prior to His painful death. He said:

> ...Father, if You are willing, remove this cup from Me; yet not My will, but [always] Yours be done.
>
> Luke 22:42 (AMPC)

Our peace of mind rests on whether or not we are willing to trust that God's will is better than ours even if we don't understand it. Because we are created with free will, we have the option of trying to run our own lives and live for what we will, but thankfully, we have another option, and that is to trust in the goodness and sovereignty of God. The prophet Isaiah puts it this way: "Of the increase of His government and of peace there shall be no end..." (Isaiah 9:7). The more we let God govern our lives, the more peace we will enjoy!

Who Is in the Driver's Seat of Your Life?

When life isn't going how we'd like, and we don't trust God, it's easy to try and take the wheel from Him, to boss Him around and try to force Him to do things our way. Sadly, this will land even the best person in an emotional and spiritual ditch. Why not let God drive your life instead?

I heard a story recently about two teenage girls who were spending the day together. One of them was a very spontaneous girl who often did things without thinking them through. She suddenly decided she wanted to trade places with the girl driving the car and proceeded to try and do so while the car was moving. Although the driver of the car initially resisted, she eventually joined in the experiment, and soon they ended up in a ditch with a damaged automobile.

I recommend letting God do the driving. Don't try to take the wheel from Him while He is taking you where He wants you to go. Let Him take the lead and learn to follow. This is the smartest, safest, and most fulfilling way to live.

This is a good place to stop reading for a few minutes and think about some questions:

- Who is in the driver's seat in your life?
- How much peace of mind do you enjoy?
- How often do you waste an entire day worrying about something that steals your peace?
- Is a fear of not getting what you want preventing you from trusting God?
- Are you hungry for more peace of mind?
- Do you want to enjoy your life more?

Answering these questions honestly may help you identify your level of trust. If you find that you are not trusting God as you should, there is no reason to be condemned. Just start from this moment to choose trust over worry. Consider this Scripture:

> You will guard him and keep him in perfect and constant peace whose mind [both its inclination and its character] is stayed on You, because he commits himself to You, leans on You, and hopes confidently in You.
>
> Isaiah 26:3 (AMPC)

Let me suggest a new way for you to pray. Instead of merely telling God what you want Him to do for you, try asking for what you want but then adding this statement: "But, Lord, if this isn't the right thing for me, then please don't give it to me!"

There have been many times in my life (and probably in yours too) when I worked hard to get what I wanted but found that it did not fulfill and satisfy me, and it even made my situation worse. Most of us have at some time purchased something that we wanted but in reality could not afford, and ended up with mental pressure because of debt. Or we may have started an argument with our spouse when there was a difference of opinion, but after getting what we thought we wanted, we realized that getting our own way wasn't worth the mental and emotional misery we experienced.

If we cannot have what we want with peace of mind, then it probably isn't worth having.

I have learned that if we cannot have what we want with peace of mind, then it probably isn't worth having. We are urged by Scripture to let peace be the umpire in our lives, making all final decisions (see Colossians 3:15). After many years of mental and emotional turmoil, I have learned that peace is a valuable commodity and we should do whatever it takes to have it.

When you find that you are having a hard time trusting God, ask yourself: "Is it because I am afraid that if I do trust Him, I might not get what I want?" If the answer is yes, then you have located the cause of your lack of trust and peace.

Getting our own way is highly overrated. It is amazing how much of our lives are wasted on the pursuit of self-gratification, only to find in the end that we are not satisfied after all.

Only God's will has the ability to ultimately satisfy us. We are created for Him and for His purposes, and anything less than that is totally incapable of bringing lasting contentment. When we are young, we may think that getting what we want is the most important thing in life, but as the years go by, hopefully we learn and have enough experience to readily say, "I want God's will more than I want my own will." There is no better place to be than in God's perfect will!

CHAPTER 3

Who Can I Trust?

…Cursed [with great evil] is the strong man who trusts in and relies on frail man, making weak [human] flesh his arm, and whose mind and heart turn aside from the Lord.

Jeremiah 17:5 (AMPC)

"You can't trust anybody these days" is a common statement, and one that most of us are tempted to make from time to time. However, it is not true that no one is trustworthy, and it's dangerous to become a cynic and think that way.

I readily admit that finding people to trust nowadays is more difficult than at any other time I can remember in my life, but I flatly refuse to live with a heart filled with distrust and suspicion. I have decided to believe the best and trust people unless they give me a definite reason not to. And this decision was not made based on my experiences with people.

I knew by the age of seven that I couldn't trust my parents because they were self-absorbed and very abusive. I couldn't trust other relatives whom I had asked to help me because they refused to do so, using the weak excuse: "I don't want to get involved; it's none of my business."

As I grew into a teenager and young adult, I had other sad experiences that screamed the message, "You can't trust anybody!"

I got married at the age of eighteen to a young man who was unfaithful, in addition to being a petty thief who ended up in prison. I am sure that I also met people who could be trusted, but I was so angry with the people who had hurt and disappointed me that I tended to focus on that.

I married Dave at the age of twenty-three, and from that point on I regularly attended church. I assumed that because I was now involved with "church people," I could trust them and would not get hurt, but that didn't turn out to be correct either. As a matter of fact, some of the deepest disappointments I have experienced in my life have come from Christians. (I can almost hear some readers saying, "Amen!") You may have experienced the same thing, and I am sure you have some harrowing stories to tell about what people have done to you.

Human beings, including ourselves, are flawed, and we are setting ourselves up for painful disappointment if we think otherwise. Jesus came for the weak, not the strong, and I am grateful that He did. I need mercy and forgiveness regularly, and that means I also need to be ready to give them generously.

The subject of trust—or rather lack of trust—fills the headlines these days. Allegations of sexual abuse by priests are reported frequently, it seems. We have heard of the Enron scandal in which thousands of people were cheated out of their life savings. We vote for politicians we think we can trust and they disappoint us by not doing what they promised.

How do we tell the good guys from the bad guys? How do we know who is trustworthy and who is not? How do we know whom we can trust? There are no easy answers, and sometimes we cannot even trust those who should be most committed to our nurturing and care. Just ask a young woman who was abused by her father, a respected deacon in his church. Everyone, including his family, believed he was the epitome of integrity and dependability. But in the end, the man proved to be deceitful and evil.

In an article titled "Who Can You Trust?" Dr. Erwin W. Lutzer says:

> Why are people untrustworthy? Though we like to think that we are driven by rational instincts, the truth is that we are driven by our own selfish desires. And because we want to be well thought of, it is easy for us to pay careful attention to our outward persona, while totally neglecting the integrity of our hearts. In fact, some people not only deceive others, but they actually end up deceiving themselves. When our self-deception is complete, we can become wicked, destroying those around us to protect our sick self.[3]

Yes, it is difficult to know who to trust. Adultery is at an all-time high. Many college students say they cheat on exams. Employees steal from their employers. And on and on the list goes. On a more minor but equally frustrating level, finding quality workmanship is getting more difficult all the time. And even something as simple as being able to trust people to keep appointments in a timely manner is rare. What are we to do?

Shall we adopt a sour and distrusting attitude and say, with everyone else, "You can't trust anyone these days"? Or should we decide to trust everyone unless and until they give us sufficient reason not to? I vote for trusting people, simply because I refuse to live with a suspicious attitude that makes me miserable just because some people may disappoint me.

Trust with Your Eyes Wide Open

We can trust people without placing a trust in them that, in reality, belongs only to God. Jesus talked about this and the apostle John recorded it:

> But Jesus [for His part] did not trust Himself to them, because He knew all [men].
>
> John 2:24 (AMPC)

This Scripture does not say that Jesus didn't trust anyone. Instead it says that He did not trust Himself to them. What does that mean? He didn't give Himself over to the idea that men would never disappoint Him. He didn't put Himself entirely in their hands for safekeeping.

> And He did not need anyone to bear witness concerning man [needed no evidence from anyone about men], for He Himself knew what was in human nature ...
>
> John 2:25 (AMPC)

Jesus was well informed about human nature and the weakness it contained. He came to strengthen men in their weaknesses and forgive their failures and sins. If we want peace in our lives, we need to do the same thing.

There is not one of us who can say that we have not hurt and disappointed others, or that we have not been hurt and disappointed. We personally experience the weakness of human nature. I never purposely mean to hurt anyone, but sometimes I do. Part of being in relationship requires a willingness to be disappointed and yet find a way to continue building trust, rather than giving up.

> *There is a difference between my being disappointed and God disappointing me.*

So I have decided to trust with my eyes wide open, and that means I don't expect anyone (except God) to never disappoint me. And even with God, I am sometimes initially disappointed when things don't turn out the way I had hoped they would. However, there is a difference between my being disappointed and God disappointing me. My own expectations are the source of my disappointment, not God, because Scripture teaches that if we put our hope in Him, He never disappoints us (see Romans 5:5).

Faulty Expectations

How much of our disappointment is someone else's fault, and how much is our own? I think that is an interesting question. I mentioned that God never disappoints. We may feel disappointed with something He does or does not do, but it is because our expectation was faulty. Instead of wanting what God wanted, we wanted what we wanted.

To expect a person to never hurt or disappoint you is a faulty expectation, simply because human nature is incapable of perfection. We want people to know what we want or how we feel, and when they don't, we are disappointed. We are disappointed that people don't understand us, but why should I fault Dave for not understanding how I feel if it is totally not in his nature to feel that way? His personality is different than mine, and some things that are really important to me don't matter to him at all, and vice versa. I can explain to him how I feel and then he can show empathy for me because he loves me, but he still doesn't know by experience how I feel, simply because he has no point of reference.

If a woman wants to be thoroughly understood, she is better off talking with another woman, and preferably one who has a similar personality. If Dave wants to discuss sports with someone who is really interested, it is pointless to talk to me. I can pretend to be interested out of respect, but I don't understand his excitement, simply because I have never felt it and probably never will.

As I write this, Dave and I have been married fifty years, and one of the reasons why our marriage has succeeded is because we learned long ago the importance of not expecting things from each other that we lack the ability to give. There are some things we can learn how to give to another person who needs it merely for the sake of kindness, but there are also some things that are impossible. Dave wants me to enjoy my life, and he knows I cannot do so unless I am free to genuinely be myself, so he celebrates who I am, not who he wishes I was. I do the same thing for him. It took us several years to get to this point, and until we did, we both experienced a lot of hurt and disappointment from the other due to faulty expectations.

Jesus knew that His disciples would disappoint Him, so He was prepared when they did and was not devastated by their actions. Judas betrayed Him, Peter denied Him, they all slept during His most crucial hour of need instead of praying with Him as He had requested, and yet He continued loving them completely. He didn't have a cynical attitude that said, "You hurt Me so I will never trust you again." He did not have a faulty expectation.

It is not wrong to expect people to do what is right and make every effort not to hurt us, but at the same time we should not expect them never to fail. People are simply not perfect!

I spent lots of years disappointed and upset most of the time because my plans didn't work out the way I had expected, until I learned that very few days ever work out exactly as I want them to. Now I plan for unplanned things, and that allows me to keep my peace.

> It is wise to plan on some unplanned things each day.

Always remember that it is wise to plan on some unplanned things each day.

Look at the Bright Side

We have talked about all the people we cannot trust, but what about the ones who have proven over and over that they *can* be trusted? As we said, nobody is perfect, but there are some amazingly outstanding people in the world who are filled with integrity and honesty. We can depend on them to keep their word and never to purposely break our trust.

I am privileged to know a few of these people and am thankful for them. When I do get hurt and am tempted to let the old "you just can't trust anybody" attitude seep back into my heart, I remember these rare people who continue to give me hope.

It is always best to look at the bright, positive side of any issue rather than the sour, negative one. One gives us peace and the other steals peace, so why not do all you can to make your life as good as you possibly can by looking at the bright side?

Discernment

There is a gift of the Holy Spirit available to us called discerning of spirits (see 1 Corinthians 12:4–11). It is a supernatural gift from God that allows us at times to be able to know who is evil and who is good. I pray often for the gift of discernment. I know that God can cause me to know something is not right with a person when there would be no natural way for me to know. I recently felt that way about someone I had just met. Each time I saw them I thought, *I don't trust you.* At first I chastised myself for being suspicious and critical, but then two different people told me on two separate occasions that the person in question was not what they appeared to be. They presented themselves as a godly person who believed strongly in living with godly behavior, but they were in fact not that way in their daily life.

I also recently experienced a feeling that something was not right with an employee. I didn't know what it was, but I just felt uncomfortable when I was with them. After a few months, we discovered that the person wasn't doing their job properly and was covering up some things that should have been brought out into the open. Because I already had sensed something wasn't right, the disappointment I felt wasn't as intense as it would have been had I been taken totally by surprise. Discernment can prevent us from getting involved with the wrong people, and it can also help prepare us for things before they happen.

When I have a feeling that something isn't right or I am uncomfortable with a person, I never rely solely on that feeling, because I know I could be wrong and I don't want to judge someone or close my heart to them based only on a feeling. But it does make me more cautious and I watch more closely. I pray that if there is a problem, God will reveal it, and He always does. Pray for discernment. It will keep you from being deceived and perhaps hurt.

A truly spiritual person is a discerning person:

But the spiritual man tries all things [he examines, investigates, inquires into, questions, and discerns all things] . . .

1 Corinthians 2:15 (AMPC)

Trust God!

Although we cannot always trust people, we can always trust God! Our Heavenly Father has proven over and over that He can be trusted with what we commit to Him.

I realize there are questions that we will need to address, such as: If God is good and He is sovereign, then why doesn't He do something about some of the horrific situations in people's lives? How can we trust someone who could do something to make our pain go away and yet doesn't? For that matter, why do bad things happen to good people? My father, who was very evil, lived to be eighty-three, and yet I recently attended the funeral of a thirty-seven-year-old Christian wife and mother of two young children. Why do evil people sometimes live a long life while the good die young?

There are some answers, but even the ones we have may not be sufficient to satisfy everyone. I will deal with these subjects to the best of my flawed ability later in the book, but once again let me say that trusting God always requires that we have some unanswered questions and still trust Him anyway. Part of trusting God without borders means that we don't stop trusting Him when we have a question with no answer! We may not know the answer, but we can rest in faith that the Lord does know.

Trusting God is a privilege; it is a choice we can make if we choose to. After lots of years of questioning many things, I have decided to trust God because there is no way for me to ever be happy unless I do. I believe He is worthy of my trust. I have experienced putting my trust in something or someone else, and I haven't found anything or anyone else flawless enough to deserve all of it, so I give it to God. I've tried trusting myself, and that was an utter disaster. I have tried trusting other people, and although there are some really good people, we have seen that human nature is flawed. The government is not a good option, nor the stock market, nor my retirement fund. After considering all my other options, God wins—I trust God!

Interestingly enough, when I wrote the last sentence, I felt a burst of joy in my soul! That tells me that God rejoices when we trust Him. He likes it, and since He lives in His people, when He rejoices, we rejoice also.

If you ever wonder where your joy has gone, check your believing. Paul told the Romans that joy and peace are found in believing (see Romans 15:13). I have tested this principle in my life and know it to be true. When I trust God, believing His Word and promises, I have peace and joy and I enjoy life. But when I don't trust Him, I am filled with doubt, fear, worry, and anxiety. It is stressful and places a heavy burden on me that I don't want to carry.

We have only two options: Trust God or don't trust God. This is not something we can do half-way and have full benefits! But as previously suggested, above all else, be honest with God. Pretense gets

> "Father, I trust You to help me learn to trust You."

us nowhere with God. If you are having trouble trusting in God but you want to trust Him, then pray this prayer: "Father, I trust You to help me learn to trust You."

God is willing to meet you where you are and help you get to where you need to be. That is the good news of the Gospel!

CHAPTER 4

The Folly of Self-Reliance

Not that we are sufficiently qualified in ourselves to claim anything as coming from us, but our sufficiency and qualifications come from God.

2 Corinthians 3:5

Trust God or trust yourself? The age-old debate takes as many turns as there are souls contemplating this question every day. Humanism has always fought hard against the thought of needing God.

Every person, and certainly every Christian, should strive to use their talents to the best of their ability, and we need to make decisions. But we are not called to run our own lives, doing as we please and ignoring God until we have an emergency that we cannot solve.

An attempt to live your life from the vantage point of self-reliance will only end in mental, emotional, and physical exhaustion, disillusionment, disappointment, the possibility of anger, and certain confusion.

Joshua 24:15 presents the choice we must make, and it is still the foremost choice for every believer:

> If it is unacceptable in your sight to serve the Lord, choose for yourselves this day whom you will serve...as for me and my house, we will serve the Lord.

Of all the cautions I could offer you today, the most important one would be, "Make your own choice about whether or not you will serve God, and don't let the world or anyone else make it for you."

Who will you trust with your one-and-only life? The Alpha and Omega, who knows the beginning from the end? Or will you trust the gods of this world system and the spirit of self-reliance?

> Who will you trust with your one-and-only life?

What Is Self-Reliance?

Self-reliance is man's attempt to attain happiness through external things such as money, position, power, appearance, property, and so on. When we are convinced that these things will make us happy, we passionately chase them, only to experience a lot of disappointment when we discover that they don't deliver what we thought they would.

I once heard someone say, "People spend their entire lives trying to climb the ladder of success, only to learn when they reach the top that their ladder is leaning against the wrong building." I doubt that anyone at the point of dying asks questions about their bank balance. They want to be with family, friends, and, hopefully, God.

I am sure you have either said or heard people say, "I don't need anybody. I am capable of taking care of myself." I said that, or something similar, for a few years in my life, but thankfully I discovered that I do need other people, and I desperately need God. People who make statements like this have usually been hurt deeply by others, and they have never been introduced to a real relationship with God through Jesus. They don't trust anyone except themselves, and they have not yet discovered that self-reliance is the worst choice they can make. They need to meet the one true God who created them and loves them unconditionally.

A person may think that they don't need anyone, but God has created us to need each other, and like it or not, we cannot function at full capacity unless we learn to lean on and partner with other people in life. As individuals, we each have talents and abilities, but not one of us has it all. God places us in relationships with others who have what we do not, and as we learn to work together, we can accomplish great things and enjoy our lives.

Sadly, we often waste time being critical of people because they don't do things the way we do, and we reject them instead of accepting them. This causes us to miss out on what they could add to our lives, and it robs them of what we could add to theirs. One of the most important things we can all learn is how valuable every person is. They are as imperfect as we are, and good relationships take work and effort, but they are definitely worth it.

Don't assume that because you've been hurt by someone, everyone will hurt you! It is better to trust and perhaps get hurt occasionally than it is to isolate yourself and refuse to open your heart to anyone. Because of my experiences with people, I built a wall around my heart and was afraid to let anyone in. I had some relationships, but they were not healthy because I spent more time trying not to be rejected than I did building good relationships. Thankfully, through my relationship with God and experiencing the power of His Word, I have learned to trust again.

> *Don't assume that because you've been hurt by someone, everyone will hurt you!*

If you have been hurt, God is waiting to heal your wounded soul. He heals the brokenhearted and gives them joy instead of sorrow (see Isaiah 61:1–7). He will become a wall of protection around you. God does not guarantee that we will never be hurt, but He does promise to comfort, heal, and restore us when we are. Take time to slowly read and ponder the following Scripture. It helped me a great deal during my years of learning how to be God-reliant instead of self-reliant.

> Blessed be the God and Father of our Lord Jesus Christ, the Father of sympathy (pity and mercy) and the God [Who is the Source] of every comfort (consolation and encouragement),
>
> Who comforts (consoles and encourages) us in every trouble (calamity and affliction), so that we may also be able to comfort (console and encourage) those who are in any kind of trouble or distress, with the comfort (consolation and encouragement) with which we ourselves are comforted (consoled and encouraged) by God.
>
> 2 Corinthians 1:3–4 (AMPC)

If I had not let God heal my wounded soul, I would not be able to teach others how to receive help and comfort from Him. God also has some important things for you to do, and people for you to help. If you are one of those who is still wounded and stuck in your past pain, I pray that you will start receiving the comfort and healing of God today. Begin by simply asking God to heal your soul and to comfort you in your pain.

God will not only heal you, He will restore the lost years of your life. He promises to give us double blessings for our former troubles if we put our trust in Him. Although this does not all happen

> God will not only heal you, He will restore the lost years of your life.

overnight, it does occur little by little as we continue trusting God and working with the Holy Spirit toward wholeness. Isaiah 61:7 (AMPC) says:

> Instead of your [former] shame you shall have a twofold recompense; instead of dishonor and reproach [your people] shall rejoice in their portion. Therefore in their land they shall possess double [what they had forfeited]; everlasting joy shall be theirs.

This promise of God has come true in my own life and for many other people I know. If it has not already been your experience, it can be. Trusting God is the key that unlocks this promise and all others as well.

The Fool

Proverbs is a book that shares principles of wisdom, and the writer, Solomon, spends a lot of time showing the outcome of both wisdom and foolishness. There are promises for both the wise man and the fool. The wise man is promised just about every blessing you could name: direction, protection, long life and good health, prosperity for the whole person, promotion, and honor, just to name a few. But the fool can expect just the opposite.

In Proverbs, the fool is often described as the self-confident or self-reliant person. Let's be clear—anyone who is self-reliant is foolish, and the outcome of such a choice is never good. A self-reliant person refuses to take advice. They are convinced that their way is always right. Shame is the highest rank that can be conferred on a fool (see Proverbs 3:35). Foolish people speak without thinking, and you can recognize them by the way they talk. They are scoffers and scorners who make fun of the righteous. They love evil and hate what is good. One of the most destructive character traits of the foolish, self-reliant person is pride. Their own pride deceives them and they refuse to listen to God.

I think it is safe to say that there are many foolish people in the world, and they will reap the fruit of their folly unless they change. The most exciting thing about God is that He offers new beginnings and fresh starts anytime we need one. No one is stuck forever in their past unless they choose to be. Although I was self-reliant for many years, with God's help I have changed, and I am very aware that I need God at all times, and I need people! I trust God to put the right people in my life, and then, together, as we put our trust in God, amazing things take place.

Even someone fully committed to being a Christian occasionally does foolish things. At least I know I do. Several months ago, I made a long-term commitment without thoroughly thinking it through, and now I wish I had not done it. I made the commitment out of emotion rather than taking the time to seek God's wisdom. I have repented and asked God to help me keep my word because I know it would be even more foolish if I didn't, and I can learn from this error in judgment.

My point is that all of us are foolish at times, but if our hearts are right with God, He can even work good out of our mistakes. Occasionally being foolish and making independent decisions without consulting God is not the same as living as a self-reliant fool.

Learning that a foolish person is described in Scripture as a self-confident or self-reliant person was eye-opening for me.

Self-reliance is a bigger problem for us than we might imagine. It basically closes the door to all the help that God wants to give us. When we rely on or trust ourselves, the result is tiny compared to the amazing result we get when we trust God!

You Don't Have to Do It All

To trust no one but yourself is a heavy burden to carry. It means that you have to do it all. Wow! I'm tired already just thinking about it, because I remember when I was that way. Part of the definition of trust is "to rely," and that means to lean on, put confidence in, depend on, or count on. When we rely on another, we immediately lighten our load.

If you hear yourself say, "I can't go on like this much longer," it probably means that you are trying to do more than what you are created for. Each of us has limits. We can recognize what those limits are if we pay attention to our stress levels. When I am carrying such a heavy load that I am worn-out all the time, complaining frequently and usually being grouchy and impatient with other people, I have gone past my limit. I need to get some help, either from God or someone He has provided. I need to rely on others, but that is hard to do if I don't know how to trust.

Do we really have to do all that we do? Are we truly the only one who can do what needs to be done? Or are we simply afraid to trust anyone else? Do we perhaps get our identity (worth and value) from being "the one who does it all"? Answering these questions with honesty requires some soul searching. We are very adept at hiding from our own selves. How many people truly know themselves and their motives behind what they do? Are we afraid to ask ourselves why we think we have to do it all because we might not like the answers we find? One of the things

I painfully discovered was that I felt I had to do it all because I was a prideful person who was convinced nobody could do what needed to be done as well as I could. (Ouch!)

I also had a root of rejection in my life from my past, and because of it, I hesitated to ask for help because I thought I might be rejected if I did. It is not comfortable when we ask for help and receive a "no" answer. Like many others, I was afraid to look below the surface of my life, so I continued doing it all until I came close to collapse. It was only then that I finally asked God for help!

If you feel that you are at the end of your rope, hold on and ask God for help. When we ask God to help us, He usually gives us some large doses of truth that are not always easy to swallow. The truth makes us free, but only if we receive it, and to be honest, that usually hurts.

It wasn't easy for me to admit I was proud, I liked being in control, I was self-reliant, or that my "I don't need anybody" attitude was ungodly. As God revealed these things to me, I felt as if my soul was being ripped open and exposed in a way that made me very uncomfortable, but the truth did set me free. And it will do the same thing for anyone who is willing to receive it.

Now I not only *don't* want to do it all, I know I cannot do it all! In reality, I never could, and neither can you.

Trusting God is the beginning of all healing. We must trust His ways even if they initially seem to make things worse. It is often hard to understand why heal-ing can hurt worse than our dis-ease, but when it comes to matters of the soul, that is often the case.

> *Trusting God is the beginning of all healing.*

I had a soul sickness. I didn't know how to trust. I lived in fear. My backpack was fully loaded with heavy burdens and I carried it continually. I am actually glad that I have my past to refer to, because it helps me see how wonderful my life is now. When I remember the pressure I lived under, and how light and free I am now, I am truly amazed at the power and goodness of God!

I talk about the way I was because I think lots of people are still stuck there. My prayer is that knowing that someone else has been set free will give a weary soul encouragement that the same thing can happen to them if they will "let go and let God" in their lives.

Lean on God and rely on Him to help you and take care of you!

I am continually shocked when I think of all the people in the world today who think they don't need God. If I didn't have God in my life every moment, I could find no purpose in anything. God designed us to need Him, so apart from God, we can never function truly well. Some may deceive themselves into thinking they have it all together, but their day of reckoning will come. They will ultimately come to the end of themselves and, hopefully, have enough humility to invite God into their lives.

If you are convicted in any way by this teaching about being self-reliant and you want help, simply ask! God is the world's top expert on helping people! His Holy Spirit is here with us and He is called the Helper (see John 14:26). Just imagine: You have a divine Helper standing by at all times, so why not give Him something to do? You really don't have to do it all. The truth is that Jesus has already done it all, and through trust, faith, and belief in Him, you can breathe a sigh of relief and let your burden go!

You can be God-reliant instead of self-reliant.

CHAPTER 5

Trust God and Do Good (Part 1)

Trust (lean on, rely on, and be confident) in the Lord and do good; so shall you dwell in the land and feed surely on His faithfulness, and truly you shall be fed.

Psalm 37:3 (AMPC)

Psalm 37:3 is a Scripture that promises that if we trust God and do good, we will be fed, but it isn't talking merely about having enough food to satisfy us. It means that we will enjoy contentment and satisfaction in our souls. We may want some things to change, but while we are waiting, we can have a soul that is satisfied in God.

Trusting God is a great benefit to the child of God. It allows him to enjoy his life rather than just surviving it. Remember that trusting God is a choice we make and it is a privilege. But there is something else that we need to add to trust in order to get the full benefit from it, and that something is "doing good."

This chapter could possibly be the most important one in the book for you. The biblical principle of Psalm 37:3 has helped me tremendously in my life, and I believe it is vital for you as well.

Trusting God means that we cast our care on Him and refuse to worry or be anxious about anything, but it does not mean that we cast our responsibility away. Quite often there is a God-inspired action we need to take in order to get what we desire. Some people have the mistaken idea that trusting in or waiting on God is passive and it means we do nothing while waiting for God to do everything, but this is simply not true. For example, someone who is trusting God to help them get a job but is not being diligent in searching for one is not likely to get a good result.

Paul said it well in his letter to the Ephesians. He said they were to do all that the crisis demanded, and then stand firmly in their place (see Ephesians 6:13). We see in this Scripture the principle of "trusting God and doing good." Do what you should do, do what you can do, and trust God to do what you cannot or should not be doing.

The first thing we always need to do is trust God in every area of our lives. The second thing we need to do is be ready to do anything that God shows us we need to do. I have been led to change how I pray when I have a need. Instead of saying, "I trust You, Lord, to do this for me," I now say, "Lord, I trust You to take care of this situation, and if there is anything I need to do, show me what it is." You may want to consider doing this unless you already do so. I think it keeps us aware of our need to listen to God for any instructions He might give us.

On January 1, 2015, I wrote in my journal that I needed and greatly desired more energy. Shortly after that, I sensed that I should start walking each day. I already work out with a trainer three days a week, but now I thought I should add walking. I leaned on God daily to give me the desire and the ability to do it. Within a few months, I was walking five miles a day and was more energetic than ever. I had more endurance and was more mentally alert. As a bonus, I also lost some weight, and although that was not my primary goal, I was thrilled. The extra cardio exercise turned out to be just what my body needed.

I trusted God to give me more energy and He gave me something to do, but He also gave me the desire and ability to do it. If you will trust God and be truly ready to do whatever He may ask of you, I guarantee that you will be amazed at the progress you make toward reaching your goals.

> I trusted God to give me more energy and He gave me something to do.

Another thing that recently happened concerned my eyes. I have extremely dry eyes and sometimes they burn and it can be really painful. I use all the eye drops that are recommended, I keep a humidifier going where I sleep, and although that helps, I was still suffering. It was especially bad when I traveled to places that have a dry climate, which I often do as part of my ministry responsibilities.

I prayed about this situation, as I had done many times before, and this time I sensed God saying that I needed to drink a lot more water than I do. I thought I was drinking a lot of water already! A couple of people had suggested that I drink more water, but because I thought I already did, I dismissed their suggestions as being irrelevant to my problem. It is interesting to note how the pride of our mind will prevent us from even considering a suggestion someone makes. We should at least ponder the advice we are given before God and see if it bears witness with our spirit. God often speaks to us through people, but we must be humble enough to listen to them.

Thankfully, God doesn't give up on us, and even though He had tried to tell me what to do through people, He was now gracious enough to tell me Himself. I felt that I ought

> Thankfully, God doesn't give up on us.

to drink twice as much as I usually did, especially when I'm in dry climates. In order to do that, I needed to drink eight sixteen-ounce bottles of water a day! Well, I set them out on a table and started drinking, and, sure enough, my eyes got better. They are not perfect, but they are certainly much better than they were before. Drinking this much water is challenging, and I have not totally mastered it daily, but I know from experience that I can form a new habit, and as I do, what is difficult now will just become part of my lifestyle.

Another time, I couldn't sleep, and after tossing and turning until the wee hours of the morning, I asked God what was wrong. He quickly called my attention to an incident that day when I had been rude and unkind to someone, and I knew immediately I needed to ask God to forgive me, and I did. I also needed to apologize to the person I had been rude to as soon as I could. I went to sleep right away after that!

My goal in life is to continue trusting God and "doing good." To do good means we do the good that God leads us to do, and we obey Him promptly in all that He reveals to us. There is also another aspect of doing good that I want to talk about in the next chapter, but let's devote this one to learning the importance of promptly following the leadings of the Holy Spirit.

Our Helper

When Jesus ascended into Heaven, He sent us another Comforter and Helper—the Holy Spirit! He said in John 14:16 (AMPC):

> And I will ask the Father, and He will give you another Comforter (Counselor, Helper, Intercessor, Advocate, Strengthener, and Standby), that He may remain with you forever.

Jesus sent His Spirit to be *with* us and *in* us at all times. The Holy Spirit is our Guide, according to John 16:13. I love the thought of having a Holy Helper to walk with me throughout my life, and I hope that thought excites you too. We never have to go it alone or do it all ourselves, because the Holy Spirit is here to help. He guides us in what to do, and He strengthens and enables us to do it! Make sure that you depend on God at all times, because apart from Him, we can do nothing (see John 15:5). When we put our confidence in Jesus and depend on Him, it removes the pressure from us.

If God wants you to take a specific action, knowing what that is may not always come quickly. But as you wait on God patiently, keeping your trust in Him, He will reveal His will. There have been times when I was waiting on God to take care of a situation and I felt my part was to speak positively about the situation and thank Him ahead of time for a breakthrough. I remember a couple of times when He asked us to give a sacrificial offering, at other times it was fasting, and still at other times He has instructed us just to worship and wait. Don't get preconceived ideas about how God works and speaks to us, because His ways are endless!

When God speaks (leads and guides), we usually sense strongly in our hearts a specific direction we are to take, or we have a thought or

> God leads those who truly want His guidance!

an idea that will not go away. God leads those who truly want His guidance! We do learn sometimes by making mistakes, so if you step out in faith and find that you misunderstood what you were to do, don't give up.

When I am doing something that God doesn't want me to do, I feel uncomfortable in my spirit and soul. If that feeling continues,

I have learned that I need to take another direction, and I wait to find out what that is. If I am doing what God wants me to, then I feel peace, grace, and joy.

Who is in control in your life? If it's God, things will work out well, but if not, they won't turn out so well.

What He Says to You, Do It!

I often tell the story of a young woman who came to me at the end of a conference and asked to speak with me. During the weekend, she had spent time with several other women who shared personal testimonies about things God had told them to do and how, after doing them, they had experienced breakthroughs they desperately needed. She said, "Joyce, everything God led them to do, He had also revealed that same direction to me. But the difference between us was they did what God told them to do so they had victory over their problems, and I did not!" Following the guidance of the Holy Spirit is the key to moving forward in life and overcoming the challenges we face.

It cannot get much plainer than that! A good biblical example is in John chapter 2. Jesus' mother wanted a miracle at the wedding of Cana when they ran out of wine. In verse 5, she turned to the servants and said to them, "Whatever [Jesus] says to you, do it." If you haven't given God total control of your life, are you willing to make this your new goal in life? If you do, you will never be sorry.

Ask yourself sincerely, "Am I really trusting God? Have I done what He has asked me to do, or am I putting off obeying Him, still hoping that I will get what I want?" Is it possible for anyone to trust God if they are not willing to obey Him? I don't think it is! That may sound a bit harsh, but I think it is true. Trusting

God is nothing more than a spiritual idea unless we trust Him enough to do what He asks us to do, and perhaps to do nothing if that is what He requires.

What if God Asks Us to Do Nothing?

There are things God asks us to do, and there are things He asks us to stop doing. There was a time when I wanted my husband to change, but God asked me to stop trying to change him! And there was a time when I wanted to change myself, but I could not do it through any amount of struggle and self-effort; I needed to wait on God, believing that He would complete the good work He had begun in me (see Philippians 1:6). I wanted to be actively involved in things that God told me to stop doing, and that was not easy for me.

Is there anything that God has asked you to stop doing? He certainly has asked me to stop doing things from time to time. I still remember how I always wanted to have the last word in a disagreement with my husband, but God told me to stop talking! I like to give my opinion, but quite often the Holy Spirit gives me the red light, signaling me to stop and reminding me to keep quiet.

I don't want any of you to frustrate yourself with works of the flesh, always trying to "do" something that you can't accomplish in your own strength or ability. Please understand that I am talking about doing what God shows you to do, or what He shows you not to do.

One of my favorite Scriptures is Psalm 46:10, which says we are to be still and know that He is God. Being still was more difficult for me than being active! God wants us to be active, but actively doing *His will*, not our own.

While you are trusting God to take care of a situation that you have committed to Him, you may sense in your spirit that He wants you to use your prayer time being grateful rather than making more requests. There are many times in life when you can do absolutely nothing except pray and wait. This is especially true when your prayer request involves something you want for a loved one. Your prayer opens the door for God to work, but the person involved still needs to let Him work in them.

There are times when I have prayed for someone for a long time and then no longer feel led to keep asking God to do something, but to thank Him that He is working!

The Power of Obedience

I talk with people fairly regularly who are confused about why their faith doesn't seem to be working. After being with them a short while, oftentimes I can see why. They complain, they are critical of others, and they are negative! That kind of behavior is not obedience to the leading of the Holy Spirit. It is vitally important for us to be obedient to God in the area of our attitudes.

We have power over our enemy, Satan, but the authority to use that power only comes through being obedient to God. Jesus was certainly powerful, but He was also obedient. Scripture says that He was extremely obedient, even unto death, and a name was given to Him that is above all other names; at the mention of His name every knee must bow (see Philippians 2:8–10).

A huge hindrance to many people seeing their prayers answered is anger and bitterness that they refuse to let go of. The subject of forgiving those who hurt us and whom we would consider "enemies" could not be any plainer in God's Word. He explicitly states that when we pray, we must forgive anyone for anything we have against them (see Mark 11:25). Therefore, if any one of us thinks we can refuse to forgive and still see God work in our lives, we are mistaken.

Now, I want to assure you I am not saying that we are saved through our obedience. It was the obedience of Christ that provides our salvation. We are saved by God's grace, not our own works! (See Ephesians 2:8–9.) Yet I truly believe that anyone who receives the gift of salvation through Christ will want to grow in the area of obedience because they love Him.

Parents expect their children to trust and obey them, so why would we think that God expects any less from us? I want to encourage you to set your mind and keep it set in the direction of trusting God at all times, doing what He asks you to do or not do (see Colossians 3:2). It is not what we do occasionally that brings victory in our lives, but what we do

> A little obedience mixed with a lot of disobedience still equals an unpleasant life.

consistently and diligently. A little obedience mixed with a lot of disobedience still equals an unpleasant life.

Will you commit to a higher level of obedience to God? If you make the commitment, He will give you the grace to do it. Are there areas that you are aware of right now that you need to release to God—not just worries and cares, but also behaviors that are not in line with His will? You can have a fresh start! A new beginning! Let the cry of your heart continually be, "Father, Your will be done and not mine!"

Now let's move on to the second part of doing good, which is so exciting I can hardly wait to share it!

CHAPTER 6

Trust God and Do Good (Part 2)

And let us not be weary in well doing: for in due season we shall reap, if we faint not.

Galatians 6:9 (KJV)

We have learned that being obedient to God and following the guidance of the Holy Spirit is "doing good." But in this chapter, I want to focus specifically on obeying God and doing good deeds by helping people who are in need.

The apostle Paul told the Galatians not to get tired of doing good (see Galatians 6:9). He instructed them to do good to all people as the occasion and opportunity opened up, especially to those of the household of faith (6:10). We should see helping other people in need as an opportunity to do good! It is an opportunity for us to bless others, and to also be blessed ourselves. People who are focused on helping others are happy people!

I sincerely believe that giving is rooted in trusting God. We do it because God has asked us to, and we believe His promise to meet our own financial needs. Doing good works does wonderful things for those who diligently practice them. Acts 20:35 (NIV) says, "...It is more blessed to give than to receive." Giving of ourselves releases joy in our lives and enables us to be happy while we wait for God to meet our own needs. So if you're wondering, "How can I be joyful when I have problems?" the answer is simple: Get your mind off yourself by focusing on doing something good for someone else. We do not have to focus on our problems all day long in order for God to give us answers. Tell Him what you want and need, and then trust Him to provide while you focus on doing good!

One of my favorite Scriptures is Acts 10:38. It says that Jesus was anointed with the Holy Spirit and "He went about doing good and, in particular, curing all who were harassed and oppressed by [the power of] the devil..." (AMPC). We are taught to imitate His behavior and follow His example, and this is one of the best ways we can do that. The world is filled with people who are oppressed by the devil, and we are anointed by the Holy Spirit to help them just as Jesus was.

Every time we do good, we are sowing a seed that will release our own harvest. Don't make the mistake of thinking that you have too many problems of your own to help other people. All that does is keep you stuck in your problems indefinitely.

> Don't make the mistake of thinking that you have too many problems of your own to help other people.

One weekend, when I was teaching on this very topic—trusting God and doing good—in one of my conferences, the power went out on the block the arena was in. It happened about an hour before the opening session, so we had to cancel it and watch thousands of people leave. The power came back on about ten minutes before the session would have been over. We had to wait and start the conference the next morning.

I had to trust God while I was trying to teach a conference

on trusting God! In addition to what we were already dealing with, the arena management lit up the billboard outside with this message: "The Joyce Meyer conference has been canceled." They thought they were helping, but they forgot to say it was only canceled that night and would start again the next morning. I had visions of being in that huge arena teaching to empty seats. I felt rather frantic in my soul but kept saying, "God, I put my trust in You," and we ended up having a great conference.

During the teaching, I used a visual prop to help people better understand the principle of trusting God and doing good. Our construction crew created two medicine bottles that were approximately three feet tall. We put them on a table and labeled one "Trust God" and the other "Do Good." The bottles also said that refills were unlimited and the patient could take them as often as needed. It is impossible to overdose on either one.

As I taught about how to handle trials and tribulations, problems and miseries of every kind, I said, "When symptoms come, immediately take a dose of 'Trust God,' quickly followed up with a dose of 'Do Good.'" This example seemed to really help people understand that doing good things for others while trusting God to be good to us is the medicine we need for our souls.

The Word of God acts as medicine for our souls if we follow what it says. Medicine doesn't help us unless we take it, and the Word of God doesn't help us if we know it but don't do it. For example, if you sin, you can do what people normally do and feel guilty and condemned, or you can take some "God forgive me" medicine and it will heal your soul. If someone has hurt or offended you, instead of being angry and upset you can take a healthy dose of "I forgive you" medicine and enjoy your day. If we look at God's Word as medicine for our souls, we find help for all of the problems we face in life.

Let me say again that I believe trusting God and doing good is medicine for our souls, and I highly recommend that you take as much as you need, as often as you need it. I should warn you, though, that there are side effects! They are peace, joy, stability, confidence, and rewards in Heaven.

What Qualifies as Good Works?

Doing a good deed can be as simple as giving a compliment or listening to someone who is hurting. It may also involve giving your time or finances to help someone in need.

The Bible is filled with Scriptures about helping the poor and needy and giving encouragement to those who are hurting. It actually says that we are to "seek" to do good deeds and acts of kindness. That means we look for ways to help others.

> See that none of you repays another with evil for evil, but always aim to show kindness and seek to do good to one another and to everybody.
>
> 1 Thessalonians 5:15 (AMPC)

Do you want to be useful in this world and live with a satisfying purpose? Charles Dickens said, "No one is useless in this world who lightens the burdens of another."[4]

God instructs us not only to help hurting people, but also to bless our enemies! Why should we do that? Because we overcome evil with good (see Romans 12:21). We have been given a secret weapon that works like a miracle when trouble comes, when people hurt us, or when we have personal needs—*do good*!

One of the first things we should do when someone hurts us or treats us unjustly is pray for them. How should we pray? Ask God to forgive them and to open their eyes so they can see how their behavior displeases Him. If they are not saved, then pray for their salvation. By doing this, you will release yourself from the misery of being angry with them and fretting over what they have done. You may not feel differently toward them right away, but it is very difficult to stay angry with someone you pray for regularly.

We should give ourselves to doing good deeds at all times, but there is a temptation to turn inward and stop reaching out when we are hurting. This is a big mistake. It is always important to do good, but it is especially important when you have problems of your own. Jesus was facing an unbelievably painful death, yet He continued being good to others by asking His Father to forgive those crucifying Him and by comforting the criminal being crucified with Him who asked for help (see Luke 23:32–43). I don't know about you, but when I am having problems of my own, it is often difficult not to be grouchy with other people. However, I have learned over the years that this is the best time to practice being kind and doing good. When we have no problems, treating others kindly requires no discipline, but it does require a great deal of discipline to trust God and continue doing His will when we are hurting.

I love Psalm 37 and read it often. Verses 1–5 give us this wisdom: Don't fret or be anxious and worried about those who do evil, because God will deal with them in His own timing. While you wait, trust in God and do good. Delight yourself in the Lord and He will give you the desires of your heart. Commit your way to Him and He will bring it to pass.

This is not just a group of Scriptures that we can read to make us feel good. They give instructions that we are to follow. When we do, not only will we end up with our needs met, but we can be a good example to people who don't know God.

It is through doing good deeds that the world will recognize that we belong to God (see 1 Peter 2:12).

It is through doing good deeds that the world will recognize that we belong to God.

The Greatest Commandment

While every command from God is great and important, Jesus said that the greatest or most important of all is that we walk in love—we are to love God and love people as we love ourselves (see Matthew 22:36–39). He also said that it is by this love that the world will know that we are His disciples:

> I give you a new commandment: that you should love one another. Just as I have loved you, so you too should love one another.
>
> By this shall all [men] know that you are My disciples, if you love one another [if you keep on showing love among yourselves].
>
> John 13:34–35 (AMPC)

We cannot discuss love without talking about doing good deeds, because that is how it is seen. Love is not just a theory or a teaching that makes a moving sermon; it is real and practical. Love can be seen and felt, and it has miracle-working power to change lives.

The world doubts our testimony simply because of all the division among us. If the church could ever unify, our testimony would be undeniable! Love finds a way to agree; it does not look for things to disagree about.

Love finds a way to agree; it does not look for things to disagree about.

A family in agreement is powerful! Dave and I learned early in our ministry that we could not be successful and have strife in our hearts. We have diligently worked hard to keep it out of our lives and have seen firsthand the power that peace and unity bring.

Don't participate in any strife in your family, home, neighborhood, church, or place of employment. It is honorable for a man to avoid strife and overlook offenses (see Proverbs 19:11). When we honor God by walking in His ways, He honors us openly in our lives.

> Love is not a feeling we have, but a choice we make about how we will treat people.

Walking in love will require us to make choices daily that will help us live beyond our emotions. We cannot do everything we "feel" like doing and obey this commandment at the same time. I may not always "feel" like taking time to be kind to someone else, but each time I do, I am walking in love. Love is not a feeling we have, but a choice we make about how we will treat people.

One Scripture that helps me to keep walking in love is Matthew 7:12 (AMPC):

> So then, whatever you desire that others would do to and for you, even so do also to and for them, for this is (sums up) the Law and the Prophets.

It is easy to see that if we always treat others the way we would like to be treated, our behavior will change. It is a simple instruction and one that we can apply to our daily lives. When a situation occurs that makes it difficult to treat someone well, just ask yourself, "What would I want this person to do for me if I was the one who needed mercy?"

Our days are often filled with minor irritations. We may be waiting for a certain parking place at the crowded mall and someone quickly pulls into the space before we can get there. Immediately we feel irritated and perhaps even outraged that they were so rude. We can yell or honk our horn, or do other ungodly things, but none of it makes us feel better, and it bring us down to their level. God will bless you in some way if you trust Him and keep doing good!

Start seeing all of these irritations and unplanned events as opportunities to show love instead of letting them make you angry.

We are given a wonderful definition of the behavior of love in 1 Corinthians 13:4-8. Please take time to look at each of these points and ask yourself if you need to grow in any of these areas:

- Love endures long and is patient and kind.
- Love is never envious nor boils over with jealousy.
- Love is not boastful or vainglorious and does not display itself haughtily.
- Love is not conceited (arrogant and inflated with pride).
- Love is not rude (unmannerly) and does not act unbecomingly.
- Love does not insist on its own rights or its own way for it is not self-seeking.
- Love is not touchy, fretful, or resentful.
- Love takes no account of the evil done to it and pays no attention a suffered wrong.
- Love does not rejoice at injustice, but rejoices when right and truth prevail.
- Love bears up under anything and everything that comes.
- Love always believes the best of every person.

- Love never quits or gives up; it is always filled with hope, and endures everything without weakening.
- Love never fails.

Helping the Poor

The Bible has a great deal to say about helping the poor, and there are some wonderful promises made to those who help them. This is one of them:

> He who has pity on the poor lends to the Lord, and that which he has given He will repay to him.
> Proverbs 19:17 (AMPC)

The apostle James said that "external religious worship [religion as it is expressed in outward acts] . . . is this: to visit and help and care for the orphans and widows in their affliction and need..." (James 1:27 [AMPC]). True religion must always be expressed with outward acts, because real Christianity affects not only the heart of man, but also his behavior. God is a giver and anyone who has a relationship with Him will also want to give. The Holy Spirit is the Helper and anyone filled with the Holy Spirit will also be a helper.

It can be a healthy exercise to ask ourselves, "What am I doing to help someone else?" Can you think of the last person you helped? Of course, we usually help our families during our daily activities, or we give gifts at Christmas, but I'm talking about something beyond that. I'm talking about living to give. A joyous and meaningful life is not found in what we get but in what we give.

A joyous and meaningful life is not found in what we get but in what we give.

How many people do we know who need help, and yet we have not even considered being the one to help them? When we start asking these difficult questions, we can find our answers to be disappointing. However, when I am disappointed in myself, I can always get "reappointed" and begin doing the right thing.

I want to encourage you to purposely help people in need. Look for them and find some way to help. It is easy to make an excuse and do nothing, but that is not the proper behavior for a Christian. Here are some of the excuses that I have made in the past or that I have heard others make:

- "I'm too busy."
- "Their problems are their own fault."
- "I have problems of my own."
- "I don't want to get involved."
- "I don't know what to do."

Instead of finding reasons why we cannot help, why not aggressively look for ways that we can help? You might know someone with a need that you cannot meet alone, but perhaps you could be the one to organize a group of people to work together to help that person. The very least each of us should do is pray and ask God to reveal to us anything He would like us to do to help the people we know who are hurting and needy. Never forget that each time you do something kind for someone else, you also help yourself.

Recently, three women attended our conference and heard me speak about the need to help dig wells in third world countries where people have no access to water without traveling hours, and sometimes a day, to get it, and when they do, it is usually dirty and diseased. We have been privileged to provide seven hundred of these wells and have watched it change entire villages.

The three women wanted to do something, so they got twenty-one families together and had a huge garage sale. At the next conference they attended, they brought an offering of over two thousand dollars to help dig a well and build a church next to it. That way we provide natural water and the water of the Word, both of which bring life!

> Give, and it will be given to you: good measure, pressed down, shaken together, and running over will be put into your bosom. For with the same measure that you use, it will be measured back to you.
>
> Luke 6:38 (NKJV)

I don't believe that our motive for giving should be to get something back. We should give because our desire is to help others, but God's Word promises that when we do, it will come back multiplied in many ways.

Job made a very radical statement. He said that if he did not use his arm to help those in need, it might as well be broken from its socket (see Job 31:16–22).

The Scriptures I am speaking of have been very impactful in my own life, and I pray you will take time to read them several times before moving on. You and I have the power to relieve suffering, and we should not let any opportunity to do so pass us by. John Bunyan said, "You have not lived today until you have done something for someone who cannot repay you."[5]

Make God Smile

It is amazing to think that we can make God smile, but Scripture says that we can. David prayed this prayer: "Smile on me, your servant; teach me the right way to live" (Psalm 119:135 [MSG]).

When we do the will of God, He smiles! I think He smiles even bigger when our obedience involves helping others, because when we do so, we are imitating Him. I've heard my son say regarding his children, "They see me do that and now they copy me." When he tells me, he is usually smiling!

Each time you put a smile on someone else's face, I think God smiles too!

CHAPTER 7

At All Times

Trust in, lean on, rely on, and have confidence in Him at all times, you people; pour out your hearts before Him. God is a refuge for us (a fortress and a high tower). Selah [pause, and calmly think of that]!

Psalm 62:8 (AMPC)

There are seventy-one verses in the book of Psalms and three in the book of Habakkuk where the word "selah" appears. Since the verse above about trusting God at all times is one of the seventy-four verses in the Bible that uses the word, I thought we should stop long enough to realize that God is saying: *This verse is very valuable and you should pause and think about it.*

In the early years of my walk with God, I focused on trusting Him to help me each time I had a problem that I felt I could not handle. But after a few years, I began to realize that I didn't have the ability to do anything without Him, so now I focus on learning to trust Him at all times. The way I do that is by living with a trusting attitude that God is my helper. Very few days go by that I don't say several times a day, "I trust You, Lord, in all things." Confessing your trust in God is a form of praise. I trust God for specific things I am aware of that are taking place in my life and in the lives of other people, but I also trust Him for "all things" that I am not aware of yet.

It is foolish to wait for an emergency or a serious problem to confront us before we decide to trust God. We can live in an attitude of trust, and when we do, we are walking by faith. This doesn't guarantee that we won't have any problems in life, but it does show that we are leaning on God to help us get through our difficulties, even if He chooses not to deliver us from them.

When Jesus was in the Garden of Gethsemane, He was aware of the difficulty, suffering and temptation that He and His disciples were about to face. He told the disciples to "pray that you will not fall into temptation" (Luke 22:40 [NIV]), but they preferred to sleep. The Scripture states that they were sleeping from grief (see Luke 22:45). Perhaps they were exhausted from worry and fear, or perhaps sleeping was their way of avoiding the problem. But Jesus spent His time praying fervently. He preemptively trusted His Father to either remove the upcoming suffering or give Him the strength to go through it.

Jesus left the choice with God. Rather than asking for His own will, He stated what He would like to have, but completed His prayer with the words, "Yet not My will, but [always] Yours be done" (Luke 22:42 [AMPC]). After He did this, an angel was sent from Heaven to strengthen Him in spirit! (See Luke 22:43.)

Our Father in Heaven is not only our Deliverer, but He is our Strengthener! If He doesn't give you deliverance right away, He will strengthen you if you are willing to be patient and continue trusting Him for the right thing at the right time.

If there are areas in our lives that we know are weaknesses for us, it would be wise to continually trust God to help us avoid temptation in those areas rather than waiting until we are in the midst of them.

One of my weaknesses for many years was either talking too

much or blurting out things without thinking. This, of course, caused problems quite frequently. I often pray in the morning before I start talking to others that God will help me be a good listener and use wisdom in all that I say.

By doing this, I am not waiting until I have already caused a problem and need to deal with the aftermath. I am praying that God will keep me from giving in to temptation when it comes. One of the wisest things we can do is know our

> One of the wisest things we can do is know our weaknesses and lean on God to grant us the strength not to give in to them.

weaknesses and lean on God to grant us the strength not to give in to them. Peter would have been much better off if he had had the wisdom to do this.

Jesus warned Peter that Satan was going to tempt him severely, but instead of asking Jesus to help him, Peter thought he was so strong, it was impossible for him to fail. Look carefully at these Scriptures and be sure the attitude that Peter displays is never your attitude:

> "Simon, Simon (Peter), listen! Satan has asked excessively that [all of] you be given up to him [out of the power and keeping of God], that he might sift [all of] you like grain,
>
> "but I have prayed especially for you [Peter], that your [own] faith may not fail; and when you yourself have turned again, strengthen and establish your brethren.
>
> "And [Simon Peter] said to Him, Lord, I am ready to go with You both to prison and to death."
>
> Luke 22:31–33 (AMPC)

Peter went on to deny Christ three times! (See Luke 22:55–61.) Perhaps if he had realized his human weakness and asked for all the help from Jesus he could possibly get, he would have been stronger. Jesus didn't want to deliver him from the temptation, but He wanted him to go through it successfully so he would have enough experience to be able to help others. But Peter obviously thought he was beyond being tempted. This was a huge mistake, and it is a mistake for any of us to think that way. Thinking more highly of ourselves than we ought to think is not wise and opens the door for our downfall (see Romans 12:3). God loves us too much not to deal with our pride so we can learn to totally depend on Him.

Paul teaches us to pray at all times, on every occasion, in every season (see Ephesians 6:18). When we do, it shows that we have our trust in God at all times.

Take time to know what your weaknesses are and be sure you are trusting God at all times to strengthen you in them. Here is God's promise to us:

> In the day when I called, You answered me; and You strengthened me with strength (might and inflexibility to temptation) in my inner self.
>
> Psalm 138:3 (AMPC)

Perhaps you feel that you have prayed for God to help you resist temptation and yet you still give in to it. I have felt that way at times, but if you will continue trusting God, you will become stronger and stronger as time goes by. Mix your trust with a thorough study of His Word to get the best result. James said that the Word contains the power to save our souls (see James 1:21).

When I pray for God to help me control the words I speak, I

also quote various verses of Scripture I have studied about the words of our mouth. My prayer sounds something like this:

> "Father, help me today speak only words of excellence. Help me be a good listener and think before I speak. I want my words to glorify You and be a blessing to those who hear them. I need You, Lord. I am nothing without You. Strengthen me in all of my weaknesses."

Then I pray and confess the Word, because reminding God of His Word is something Isaiah said we should do (see Isaiah 43:26). Surely God doesn't forget His Word, so why should we remind Him of it? Here are some reasons:

- When we remind God of His Word, it shows that we are putting our trust completely in Him and in His promises.
- Speaking the Word out loud is a very powerful thing to do because it is the sword of the Spirit that is one of our weapons of spiritual warfare (see 2 Corinthians 10:4–5; Ephesians 6:17).
- Speaking God's Word helps continue the process of renewing our minds (see Romans 12:2). It is part of the process of meditating on God's Word, and that is something we are often encouraged to do in Scripture.

Here are three of my favorite Scriptures regarding the words of my mouth that I often include in my prayer:

> Set a guard, O Lord, before my mouth; keep watch at the door of my lips.
>
> Psalm 141:3 (AMPC)

Let the words of my mouth and the meditation of my heart be acceptable in Your sight, O Lord, my [firm, impenetrable] Rock and my Redeemer.

Psalm 19:14 (AMPC)

Death and life are in the power of the tongue, and they who indulge in it shall eat the fruit of it [for death or life].

Proverbs 18:21 (AMPC)

You may use this same idea of prayer and confessing the Word of God in any area in which you need help. Is your weakness anger? Overeating? Selfishness? Whatever it is, I can promise you there are Scriptures that are promises in God's Word that cover it. Using Bible programs that are readily available these days on the Internet makes this easy to do. Also, I strongly urge you to remember that it is not what we do right one or two times that brings victory into our lives. Be committed to continue leaning on God and His Word first and foremost *at all times* and you will see change in due time.

Continual Contentment

If we trust God at all times, then naturally that means we trust God in things we don't understand and that don't seem fair just as much as we do at other times. It is one thing to trust God when we get what we want, but quite another to trust Him when we don't. I believe that our goal as Christians should be to say with the apostle Paul, "I have learned

> *It is one thing to trust God when we get what we want, but quite another to trust Him when we don't.*

how to be content...in whatever state I am" (Philippians 4:11 [AMPC]). Paul said he had learned how to be satisfied to the point where he was not disturbed whether he had plenty or was in need (see Philippians 4:11–12).

Being content does not mean that we never want to see any change, or that we have no vision for better things, but it does mean that we are not allowing the things we want and don't have yet to steal the enjoyment of what we have at the present time.

I had quite a few years that were very frustrating, and the root of the problem was that I was not enjoying where I was on the way to where I was going. God is all for progress and growth, but even more than that, He is for peace!

Consider this Scripture from the book of Ecclesiastes:

> Better is the sight of the eyes [the enjoyment of what is available to one] than the cravings of wandering desire. This is also vanity (emptiness, falsity, and futility) and a striving after the wind and a feeding on it!
>
>   Ecclesiastes 6:9 (AMPC)

The writer (who is believed to be Solomon) is saying that it is vanity (useless and pointless) to so strongly desire what you don't have, and it prevents you from enjoying what you do have.

Paul had learned to be content whether he got what he wanted or he didn't, and this must be our goal. To only be content and thankful when we get our own way is very childish and does not display spiritual maturity at all. As parents, we correct our children for this type of immature behavior. We remind them of all their blessings and tell them to be thankful for what they have. Perhaps we need to remember to also set an example for them to follow in the way we behave when we don't get what we want.

Trusting God is easy when everything goes our way; however, this book is about learning to trust God *at all times*.

Being content when life hurts, or when we have to wait and don't understand why, requires a belief that God is good and that His ways are different than our ways. What I would do for myself might not be the best for me. I am sure it would feel good and seem to be good at the time, but would it help me long-term? Would getting my way all the time help me be less selfish, more loving, more understanding, and more compassionate with others when they are hurting? No, it would not! The only way to truly identify with others is to have some experience dealing with the types of things they are dealing with. We don't have to go through everything everyone experiences in order to help them, but we cannot understand disappointment, or emotional pain, or physical pain, or any other difficulty if we have never experienced it.

We turn to Jesus in our pain because He is a High Priest who understands our weaknesses and infirmities. How can He understand? He understands because He has been tempted in all points just as we are and yet He never sinned (see Hebrews 4:15). It is easy for us to go to Jesus for help because we believe He understands us! He is acquainted with sickness and grief, pain and rejection. Just as we can come to Jesus, we should also want it to be easy for others to come to us with the same confidence, believing we will understand.

As we go through things in life, those experiences equip us to be used by God to bring comfort and encouragement to others who are in need. We may not (and probably won't) always understand God's ways (see Isaiah 55:9), but we can honor Him by continuing to believe He is good and that His ways are always right!

Trust Requires Patience

Trusting God always requires patience, because God doesn't work on our timetable. Patience allows us to enjoy life while we

> Patience allows us to enjoy life while we wait!

wait! It may be difficult for us to understand why God doesn't do something that we know He could easily do if He chose to, and when this happens, He of course has His reasons. It may be to test our faith or to stretch our faith so our capacity to live by faith grows. It may be that God wants to do something better than what we want or presently have the ability to handle. All of these reasons (and many others) are opportunities for us to remain peaceful by trusting God's sovereignty, His goodness, and His wisdom.

Patience is usually not a fruit of the Spirit that is easy to have an abundance of in our lives. I find that I am patient in some areas and not in others, and I am certainly still growing in patience. We all wait for things, so waiting is not an option, but how we behave and the attitude we have while we wait is an option. The fruit of patience is partially defined in *Vine's Expository Dictionary* as a fruit of the Spirit that grows only under trial. Wow! Don't you wish it said something else? I know I do!

I would like to just pray for more patience and have God download it into me, but it doesn't work that way. We have the fruit of patience in us as children of God, but it must be developed and allowed to work its way from the inside of us to the outside of us. It needs to be more than a spiritual theory, or idea; real patience functions in our everyday life and situations. And we especially need patience when we have to wait on something that we want right now!

Whether we are waiting in line at the market, waiting in traffic, waiting for a person who is late for an appointment, or waiting on God to answer our prayers, we definitely need patience in this life if we want to have peace and enjoy our lives. Saint Augustine said, "Patience is the companion of wisdom."[6] Patience may seem bitter and sour, but its fruit is sweet.

Quite often the reason God is requiring us to wait is simply that He is using our difficulty to work patience in us. Learning to be patient is important enough to God that He restrains Himself from giving His children what they want immediately. This is something many parents need to learn. Sadly, our world is filled with people who have not been taught this very important principle in their lives, and they now demand instant gratification. The desire for instant gratification causes us to make many unwise decisions. For example, some people get into deep debt that causes great stress in their lives. And some people marry someone who is wrong for them because they are following unbridled emotions. The misbelief that we should have instant gratification fuels unhappy lives and many bad attitudes, as well as bad choices.

Knowing the nature of God, I doubt that He keeps anyone waiting unless He knows it will be the best thing for them. It is difficult for us to believe that waiting is good for us, but that is due to faulty training and the nature of the flesh. Waiting is good—it makes us more thankful when we finally get what we desire.

Impatience adds pressure to our lives, but trusting God while we wait removes that pressure and allows us to wait with an attitude that glorifies Him. The benefits of trust are truly beautiful. When we believe that God is taking care of something that is troubling us, it frees us up to focus on other things that will bear good fruit. It aids in good health and long life, and I believe even helps us to be easier to get along with. Trust removes frustration and stress from our lives, and those are two of the major sources of being grouchy and irritable with other people. We don't necessarily want to hurt people and treat them unkindly, but when our souls are filled with turmoil, we simply are more focused on how *we feel* than on how we are treating other people. We often don't even realize how harsh and rude we are being, but people feel it, and they eventually will avoid us if the abuse continues.

I absolutely love having the privilege of trusting God! And I also absolutely despise being worried, fearful, frustrated, and overloaded with stress! If you are making a decision about which way to go in your current situation and how to approach your life, I can guarantee you that trusting God is the best option.

CHAPTER 8

If God Is Good, Why Do People Suffer?

I consider that our present sufferings are not worth comparing with the glory that will be revealed in us.

Romans 8:18 (NIV)

The subject of suffering is one of the most difficult to teach on, so I approach it with much prayer and would like to start by saying that I do not in any way feel that I have all the answers. However, I cannot write a book on trusting God if I don't deal with the subject, because one of the most frequently asked questions is, "If God is good, why do people suffer?"

As Christians, we may not question why unbelievers suffer— after all, if someone does not believe in God, perhaps we can understand their suffering. So our question becomes, "Why do Christians suffer?" We are taught to believe that God loves us and wants us to have a peaceful and joyful life, and He does, but He also teaches us that we can have that in the midst of suffering.

I hear questions like:

- "Does God cause suffering?"
- "Does God allow suffering?"
- "If God is sovereign, then why doesn't He stop suffering?"

- "Why does He allow hunger, abuse, disease, and thousands of other conditions that cause suffering?"
- "Why do children sometimes suffer with cancer?"
- "Why do the good sometimes die young?"
- "Why did I lose my job and all of my retirement?"
- "Why doesn't God do something about famine or genocide?"

> *I do know that God is good, so I choose to focus on that instead of what I don't fully understand.*

"Why?" can almost drive a person to insanity if they cannot come to terms with it. If I were to answer those questions, I would start by simply saying, "I don't know." I *do* know that God is good, so I choose to focus on that instead of what I don't fully understand. I believe a firm assurance of God's goodness allows us to deal with personal suffering and the suffering around us without falling captive to confusion. If going into a room and screaming, "Why, God? Why did this happen?" helps you, then go ahead and do it. But be prepared for the probability of not getting an answer and still being left with the choice of either trusting God or frustrating yourself unbearably.

I must admit that I spent the first several years of my walk with God asking "why?" about everything I did not understand, but I also spent a lot of time in confusion and frustration. My unanswered questions were adversely affecting my relationship with God, so I finally stopped demanding answers from Him and decided to trust Him totally, especially when I was suffering or did not understand what was happening in my life.

After suffering terribly for fifteen years due to sexual abuse from my father, and then another twenty-five years or more from the effects of that abuse, I can tell you that I had lots of questions. As a child, I prayed and asked God to get me out of the situation

I was in, but He did not. Although He didn't deliver me from it, He did give me the strength to get through it and the grace to recover from it. All too often, we look at what God has *not* done for us instead of what He *has* done.

I think that is one of the biggest mistakes we can make! You can decide to rejoice over what you do have instead of grieving over what does not seem fair or just in your life. Don't let something you don't understand blind you to the goodness of God.

> *All too often, we look at what God has not done for us instead of what He has done.*

I don't believe that God always keeps us in the dark concerning why things happen or don't happen, but there certainly are many things hidden in the unfathomable wisdom of God—things that are past finding out and that will remain mysteries to us until we go to Heaven. Consider this Scripture:

> Oh, the depth of the riches and wisdom and knowledge of God! How unfathomable (inscrutable, unsearchable) are His judgments (His decisions)! And how untraceable (mysterious, undiscoverable) are His ways (His methods, paths)!
>
> Romans 11:33 (AMPC)

God promises to give us insight into mysteries and secrets as we seek Him (see Ephesians 1:17), and yet we are also told by the apostle Paul that we only know "in part," and we won't know all things until we are with Jesus, face-to-face (see 1 Corinthians 13:9–10).

I often say that trust requires unanswered questions. God reveals many things to us and gives us answers to complex problems, but

> *Trust requires unanswered questions.*

there are times when we could not receive the answer to a situation even if God gave it. I don't believe our finite minds are capable of grasping some things that only God knows. And I firmly believe that He shows us what is right for us to know and hides things that are not.

We live life forward and yet we often can only understand it by looking back. There are many painful things I did not understand when they were happening to me. But now as I look back, I see things differently than I did before, because I see the good that has come from the previous pain I endured or because I have grown spiritually. David said, "My heart is not proud, Lord, my eyes are not haughty; I do not concern myself with great matters or things too wonderful for me" (Psalm 131:1 [NIV]).

I think David was simply saying that there are things hidden in the mysteries of God that no man can possibly understand. Perhaps we should ask fewer questions and simply trust God more! I love this statement I heard by Lee Strobel: "God's ultimate answer to suffering isn't an explanation; it's the incarnation."[7] God sent Jesus to suffer and die for our sins. He has promised deliverance to all those who trust in Him, but He never tells us exactly when or how our deliverance will come. Until it does, we have the privilege of trusting God and receiving His comfort all through our difficulties.

When we see a loved one die from an illness at a young age, we may say, "Their deliverance never came, so how can I believe that God always delivers us?" I stand firm that He does always deliver those who trust in Him. It may not always be while we are here on this earth, but once we join Him in Heaven, there is no more pain, tears, or suffering of any kind.

I once heard a powerful story about a young man who fell down a flight of stairs as a baby and shattered his back. He had been in and out of hospitals his whole life. By the age of seventeen, he had spent thirteen years of his life in hospitals. He said that he thought God was fair, and when he was asked, "How can you possibly think that?" he replied, "Well, God has all eternity to make it up to me."

It is difficult to explain exactly what I feel in my spirit when I hear stories like this or meet people who have endured terrible suffering and yet they still trust God. All I can say is that I sense beauty in their trust, and they are a great example of someone who has faith in God in all seasons of their life. It is one thing for a person to trust God when things are going their way and their prayers are quickly answered, but it is quite another to trust God when you are suffering or have prayed, perhaps for a long time, and you're still waiting for a breakthrough. My opinion is that it requires a much greater faith to do the latter.

Is God Good?

Yes, God is good! His very nature is goodness and He cannot be otherwise. Merely because a thing doesn't seem good or feel good to us doesn't mean that God is not good. There are about seven hundred Scriptures that tell us God is good. I like this verse in James:

> Every good gift and every perfect (free, large, full) gift is from above; it comes down from the Father of all [that gives] light, in [the shining of] Whom there can be no variation...
>
> James 1:17 (AMPC)

Everything good comes from God—that is absolutely all that He is capable of, and there is no variation of that truth. I am sure when I say that, there are some readers who may wish to say back to me, "If God is always good, then why do people suffer?" There are many reasons why we suffer, but none of them are because God arranged it. He is not the author of suffering, Satan is! Although a thing may not be good in and of itself, because God is good, He can work good out of any situation in our lives. You might have, or know of, a situation that is so terrible it makes you think, *There is no way that anything good can come of this*, but all things are possible with God.

I can say without hesitation that God has taken the abuse I suffered as a child and worked it out for my good and the good of many others whom I have had the privilege of teaching. That understanding did not happen when I was bitter and filled with self-pity and hatred for my abusers. It began to happen little by little as I trusted God to take the bad thing and work good out of it. The same thing can happen for you. I urge you to trust God at all times because I believe it is the only option that will produce the help you need. If we don't trust God, we have nothing left but confusion and bitterness over all the tragic things we witness and experience in life.

God is good, and what He does is good (see Psalm 119:68). So is it possible that suffering can ever be for our good? Once we are afflicted with suffering, is it possible that God might take longer to deliver us than we would like for Him to because He intends to use the bad thing to work some good in us? Of course it is very possible, and most of us can testify that wonderful things have happened in us as a result of things we have gone through that we would rather not have experienced. Given the choice, we would avoid all suffering, but we are not always given the choice; however, we do have a choice as to whether or not we will trust God to work something good out of it.

I want to discuss this in much more detail later, but before we can make progress in trying to grasp the meaning of at least some of our suffering, we must have a foundation in our hearts of an unquestionable belief that God is good and He does good things. In the beginning, after He had created the things we now enjoy, He looked at it all, and Genesis 1:31 (AMPC) states, "God saw everything that He had made, and behold, it was very good (suitable, pleasant) and He approved it completely..."

Some people have asked the question, "If God is good, then why didn't He create a world without suffering and tragedy?" Actually, He did! All we need to do is look at the Garden of Eden and the original plan God had for man and we can see that everything was good. However, God gave man free will, and, sadly, the result has been suffering. He wants us to love Him freely, not as puppets who have no choice in what they do. He wants us to use our free will to choose His will. Adam and Eve did not choose the will of God, and the result was that pain entered the world. Jesus came to deliver us from the tragic choice of Adam and Eve, but we will not see the fullness of what He did until we go to Heaven. Paul said in Ephesians that the Holy Spirit we have received "is the guarantee of our inheritance [the down payment on our heritage], in anticipation of its full redemption and our acquiring [complete] possession of it..." (Ephesians 1:14 [AMPC]).

That Scripture reveals a lot to us. When we receive Jesus as our Savior and Lord, things in our lives get better. And the more we learn of

> God delivers us from our enemies little by little.

Him, and how to walk in obedience to His will, the better they get. Solomon said that the path of the righteous grows brighter and brighter until the full light of day (see Proverbs 4:18). And

Deuteronomy 7:22 says that God delivers us from our enemies little by little.

Even the earth groans, waiting for the full redemption of the children of God. This Scripture brings that truth out in a powerful way:

> And not only the creation, but we ourselves too, who have and enjoy the firstfruits of the [Holy] Spirit [a foretaste of the blissful things to come] groan inwardly as we wait for the redemption of our bodies [from sensuality and the grave, which will reveal] our adoption (our manifestation as God's sons).
>
> Romans 8:23 (AMPC)

We now have a foretaste of the goodness of God, but the day will come when we will enjoy it fully. As long as there is sensuality, there will be sin, and as long as there is sin, there will be suffering. God has never promised to deliver us from all suffering while we are in the earth, but He has promised that we can enjoy His resurrection power which lifts us above it (see Philippians 3:10). In other words, He enables us to bear it with joy and composure. Jesus told us that in the world we would have tribulation, but we should cheer up because He has overcome the world (see John 16:33).

I am enjoying the goodness of God as much as possible while I am here on earth, and I look forward to even better things when I am no longer in my body and am at home with the Lord. Until that day comes, I pray I will never say anything other than, "God is good!" No matter what we may suffer, or how many tragedies we see in the earth, they are *not* God's fault—God is good!

Suffering Is Not Permanent

One of the most encouraging things to remember when you are suffering is that it won't last forever. At least it won't for those who believe in Jesus, because no matter how bad things are here in the earth, we can look forward to eternity with God where we are promised no more pain of any kind.

> God will wipe away every tear from their eyes; and death shall be no more, neither shall there be anguish (sorrow and mourning) nor grief nor pain any more, for the old conditions and the former order of things have passed away.
>
> Revelation 21:4 (AMPC)

Most things that are painful are resolved before we die and go to Heaven, but even if we look at the extreme possibility of a lifetime of suffering, even that will end and be replaced with unimaginable enjoyment.

This too shall pass is the way to think when you are hurting, because it helps you not to feel overwhelmed. Recently I had a sinus infection that caused a headache that lasted thirty-five days. I said very often, "This too shall pass," and it eventually did. But when we have been suffering for a while, we usually start to think, *This is never going to end.* Yet most things do eventually end. Broken hearts heal, or at least they can if we let Jesus work in our lives. Psalm 147:3 (NIV) says, "He heals the

Injuries heal, disappointments turn into new dreams, and the end of one thing opens the door for the beginning of another.

brokenhearted." Injuries heal, disappointments turn into new dreams, and the end of one thing opens the door for the beginning of another.

All of us can look back over our lives and recall many circumstances that were very painful, and yet those things have been resolved and we're no longer suffering because of them. For thirty years I had chronic pain in my back that limited the things I could do. Two years ago, I saw a new doctor, and he was wise enough to send me for a test I had never had. It was discovered that I had what was probably a birth defect in my hip that was causing my back problems. Through the amazing technology available today, I had a hip replacement and no longer suffer from back pain. I can do many things I previously could not do. One would think that if they had the same problem for thirty years it was a permanent situation, but in my case, it had an end that gave me a new beginning.

I don't think we should ever give up our hope of recovering from any type of suffering. The hope of improvement is much better than being hopeless! Can your heart ever heal from the sudden and devastating loss of a loved one? Yes, because God is the God of all comfort and all things are possible with Him.

The apostle Paul experienced suffering beyond what most of us will ever have, and yet he referred to it as a light, momentary affliction:

> For our light, momentary affliction (this slight distress of the passing hour) is ever more and more abundantly preparing and producing and achieving for us an everlasting weight of glory [beyond all measure, excessively surpassing all comparisons and all calculations, a vast and transcendent glory and blessedness never to cease!]
>
> 2 Corinthians 4:17 (AMPC)

Paul had the attitude that is available to us as we choose to trust God. He stated that he looked not to the things that he could see, but to the things that he could not yet see (see 2 Corinthians 4:18). In other words, Paul looked at life in the spirit rather than in the flesh. He believed in the goodness of God even in the midst of his suffering, and he believed, according to the Word of God, that he would spend eternity in a glorious place where all of his suffering would be turned to bliss.

CHAPTER 9

Does God "Allow" Suffering?

Whatever the Lord pleases, that has He done in the heavens and on earth, in the seas and all deeps.

Psalm 135:6 (AMPC)

One might say, "I don't believe God causes suffering and tragedy. I don't believe He is the author of it, but does He allow it? If He does allow it, what is the purpose, and what is the difference between Him allowing it and Him doing it? How can I trust a God who might allow me to suffer evil and tragedy?" I know these questions exist, because people have asked me to answer them.

I have also heard someone say, "It is not science that has caused me not to believe in the existence of a supreme being, it is all the suffering and evil in the world." This man could not reconcile the evil he saw with the existence of a God who is said to be good. For some of us, faith transcends all of these questions, but many other people require an answer in order to believe.

It was the pain I experienced from an evil father that drove me to faith in God. The pain and suffering was more than I could live with, and I found peace, hope, and healing through my relationship with God. The benefits I have received from knowing and believing in God have far outweighed the questions I've had, and now I'm able to set them aside until the day comes when I either receive answers from God or I am with Him in Heaven where the answer to every question will become clear.

However, I understand the questions people ask, and I don't think it is wrong to ask them. God is not offended by our questions, but He doesn't always see fit to answer them. No matter how many questions are answered for us, there will always be others that require us to decide whether or not we'll trust God even when life doesn't seem to make any sense.

I will do my best to try and answer the question of whether or not God "allows" suffering, but I want to state ahead of time that my answers will be imperfect, especially for the person who is looking for an excuse not to believe in God. They will also be unsatisfactory to the person who feels they must be able to mentally understand all things. Our search for knowledge is good, but it can also be our undoing if it is carried too far. A lifetime Scripture for me is found in Proverbs:

> Lean on, trust in, and be confident in the Lord with all your heart and mind and do not rely on your own insight or understanding.
>
> In all your ways know, recognize, and acknowledge Him, and He will direct and make straight and plain your paths.
>
> Be not wise in your own eyes . . .
>
> Proverbs 3:5–7 (AMPC)

Peace is never found in relying on our own understanding. *Why did this or that happen, and why did it happen to me?* is the first deceptive thought our enemy, Satan, whispers to us in his efforts to draw us away from relationship with God. We can go all the way

> Peace is never found in relying on our own understanding.

back to the Garden of Eden and read how he whispered questions to Eve that eventually led Adam and her into sin that changed the course of God's desired plan for man. Satan said to her, "Can it really be that God has said, 'You shall not eat from every tree of the garden'?" (Genesis 3:1 [AMPC]). The question opened the way for another question that Satan did not even need to ask—*If all the fruit of the trees in the garden is good, why would God want to withhold any of it from me?* Eve then began to reason, and her reasoning led to deception that altered the course of her life.

God created a world that was perfect and without suffering and tragedy. He wanted Adam and Eve to function with authority and subdue the earth, using all of its vast resources in the service of God and man (see Genesis 1:28). It was not God who invited suffering into the world; it was the man and woman He created. As soon as they listened to Satan instead of God and ate the fruit God had told them not to eat, their suffering began. With one decision, they went from freely living in and enjoying the love and fellowship of God to hiding from Him in fear (see Genesis 3:8).

God is sovereign, and of course He can do anything, anytime, anywhere, and to anyone He chooses. We pray, and those prayers are dependent on the sovereignty of God. We depend on the promise that with God, all things are possible (see Matthew 19:26). However, God made a choice to give man free will, and that changes the dynamics of whether or not we will suffer evil. Will we obey God, or will we go our own way?

God loves us and wants us to love Him, but love is not true love if it is forced. It must be freely given to have any meaning. We always give freedom to those we truly love. I heard it put like this: Love demands free choice, and where there is free will, there will always be evil, but where there is evil, there can be a Savior, and where there is a Savior, there can be redemption, and where there is redemption, there can be restoration.

God gave man free choice with the foreknowledge that he would choose poorly and that his choice would open the door for pain and suffering, but God did not leave us without an option and without help. From this viewpoint, God allowed suffering to enter the world, but even that was better than creating a man who was a puppet with no choice as to whether or not he would love or how he would behave.

God never has a problem in which there is no answer! Knowing what would happen, He planned from the very beginning of time to send His only Son, Jesus, to pay for sin and open a way for God to have relationship with His children once again. God has not provided an escape from suffering, because sin is still present in the world and as long as there is sin, there will be suffering. But through Jesus, God has provided forgiveness for sin, comfort, grace, strength, and all the help we need to bear with suffering patiently when we must do so. He has gone even further and said that if we trust in Him, He will cause even our greatest suffering to work for our good:

> We are assured and know that [God being a partner in their labor] all things work together and are [fitting into a plan] for good to and for those who love God and are called according to [His] design and purpose.
>
> Romans 8:28

A thing doesn't have to be good in order for good to be worked from it. This, in itself, is proof that God is good and that His goodness can swallow up all the ill effects of injustice and personal suffering. If

A thing doesn't have to be good in order for good to be worked from it.

for no other reason than this, we should make the choice to trust God. With or without faith in God, we will experience suffering in this life. Jesus told us that in the world we will have tribulation, but He followed that fact with this amazing promise: He has overcome the world (see John 16:33). Sin caused suffering, and Jesus is the answer to it! God has not left us helpless!

If we will suffer without God, then why not suffer with Him, trusting Him to either deliver us from it at the right time or to work good out of it? To me, it only makes sense to trust God. Trusting God opens the possibility of our receiving help, whereas not trusting or believing in God dooms us to suffering without the hope of deliverance or healing.

God works all things together for good to those who love Him, trust Him, and want His will! We are born with free choice, and when we suffer, we also have the choice to trust God or not to trust Him.

All Suffering Is the Result of Sin

If there were no sin, there would be no suffering. All suffering and evil is the result of sin. It may be a direct result of our own sin or someone else's, or an indirect result of living in a fallen world. Satan is the author of sin. He is the tempter and the deceiver, so we can rightly say that Satan is the source of our problems, but we must also take some responsibility by realizing that whom we listen to and follow still comes down to our free will. Will we believe in and obediently listen to God's instructions for our lives, or will we let sensuality rule us through the lies of Satan? Satan offers us temporary pleasure that appeals to our emotions, just as he did with Eve, but God offers us a life that goes far beyond a bit of temporary pleasure. He offers us right relationship with Him, peace, joy, and a meaningful life through participation and fellowship with Him.

Let me caution you not to try too hard to link up your suffering with some personal sin. Many a sick person has increased their misery by falling prey to guilt over what they may have done wrong to open the door for their sickness. Although we may open the door for sickness through personal sin, it is also quite possible that we did nothing wrong to cause the problem and that it is simply the result of living in a sinful world where sickness and disease are some of the resulting effects. Don't persecute yourself with guilt when you are already suffering from some other tragic or painful event. Even when God chooses to show us that we have done something wrong, He doesn't make us feel guilty in the process. God convicts us; He offers an opportunity for us to repent and receive His forgiveness. God does not condemn us; that is the work of the devil.

Even more than wanting to know why people suffer and why the world is filled with evil, people want to know what their purpose is in life. They want to feel that they have value. The problem with man is not suffering, but such excessive pleasure that it no longer satisfies him in any way. A country like India, for example, is filled with every kind of suffering, and it is very religious. Even though it is filled with false religions, its people seek for God. They believe in worshipping something other than themselves. But the Western world, which was birthed out of a great faith in God, has enjoyed every kind of pleasure, and yet it seems to be moving farther and farther away from Him. In essence, the Western world has told God that He is no longer welcome. As nations, we are turning to humanism, which is man in control without

God. And the more sin abounds, the more suffering and evil will abound. But no matter how much a nation turns away from God, any individual who will turn to Him, trusting Him in all things, will experience the beauty of receiving God's help in their difficulties. That person will also experience deliverance and a great deal of protection from evil, but Scripture never makes the promise that we can avoid it altogether. We are in the world and the world is filled with sin; therefore, we cannot avoid all of its effects.

Suffering can be divided into two categories. The first is suffering that results from moral decisions, and the second is natural suffering, which includes natural disasters like floods, fires, storms, and the like. Are these disasters from God or allowed by God? Some theologians think they are, and others think they are not. Rather than enter into a theological debate over that, I prefer to see disasters as the earth groaning under the weight of sin.

There are always good and innocent people who are devastated by loss and suffer as a result of natural disasters. I prefer to try and help those people, rather than debate why the disasters happened in the first place. There are people who believe in and trust God, and yet they are affected adversely by natural disasters just as evil people are, and these are things that we cannot explain—at least I can't. But those who trust God can have the hope of help and restoration. Mercy and kindness always triumph over judgment.

When Will Help Come?

It seems that God helps me sometimes and at other times He doesn't. Although it may *seem* that way to me, it is not the case. When God doesn't give me the help I want, the way I want it, knowing God's character helps me to trust that He always helps me in the way that's best for me when I ask Him to. We are often so intent on getting what we want that we may feel that if God is not giving it to us, then He is not helping us at all. Too much preoccupation with self-will may cause us not to see what God is doing to help us.

Then we have the issue of timing. Sometimes we pray and God helps and delivers us right away, but at other times His help comes on a timetable we do not understand. If I am going through something that causes me to suffer, and God is going to deliver me, then why wait for months or even years before doing so? He always has His reasons, but He rarely shares them with us. He uses our suffering at times to work something in us that we would not allow Him to do during our good times.

C. S. Lewis said, "Pain insists on being attended to. God whispers to us in our pleasure, speaks in our consciences, but shouts in our pains. It is his megaphone to rouse a deaf world."[8]

When we do hear from God, it is not necessarily the first time He has spoken to us. I have found that sometimes my own thoughts on a matter prevented me from receiving the thoughts of God, which were quite different from mine. I mentioned earlier that God's answer to my dry eyes was for me to drink more water, but since I already thought I drank a lot of water, I wasn't receiving His answer. I look back now and realize that He used several people to say, "Perhaps you need to drink more water," but I was quick to answer, "I already drink a lot of water; that is not the answer!"

There is a man in 2 Kings chapter 5 named Naaman. He was commander of the Syrian army, a mighty man of valor, but he was a leper. A message came to him through a maid that the prophet Elisha could heal him, so they took Naaman to Elisha with a letter from the king of Syria asking him to help the commander. When Naaman arrived, Elisha did not personally talk with him but sent a message to him that he should go and wash in the Jordan River seven times and he would be healed. Naaman became angry and left because he "thought" the man of God would come out to him and, with great ceremony, heal him. It seems that because he was a great commander, he was accustomed to being treated royally, but that was not to be the case this time.

The Bible says that Naaman went away in a rage, stating that if he had wanted to wash in a river, he had no need to travel that far to do so because there were better rivers where he lived. But one of his servants said to him, "My father, if the prophet had bid you to do some great thing, would you not have done it?" (2 Kings 5:13 [AMPC]). God used this lowly servant to challenge Naaman's pride, which was the very thing preventing him from receiving the healing he desperately needed. How often do we "think" something should be a certain way and when God offers us another way (His way) we dismiss it because we don't understand it or may even be offended by it?

God's Word says, "...Let every man be quick to hear [a ready listener], slow to speak, slow to take offense and to get angry" (James 1:19 [AMPC]). I think we might receive some of the answers we need if we will listen a little better than we usually do. At least I know that is the case for me.

I frustrated myself a great deal as a younger and more immature Christian because I always wanted to know the "why" behind everything I didn't like or understand. *God, why is it taking so long for my ministry to grow? Lord, I'm praying, so why aren't You changing Dave and my children?* The answer is obvious to me now: He wasn't changing my ministry or my family because *I* was the one who needed to change; I just wasn't mature enough to realize it at the time. These experiences taught me that God sometimes waits to answer because we are asking the wrong question, and sometimes we are not ready to receive what we are asking for.

> *God sometimes waits to answer because we are asking the wrong question.*

The bottom line is, no matter what the question may be, the answer is always the same: Trust God!

CHAPTER 10

Reasons Why We Suffer (Part 1)

Thank [God] in everything [no matter what the circumstances may be, be thankful and give thanks], for this is the will of God for you [who are] in Christ Jesus...

1 Thessalonians 5:18 (AMPC)

Although we will never understand suffering completely, there are things we can learn about it, and it is wise to do so. When we understand something, it is usually easier to bear with it than if we are totally confused by it. When we have no understanding, it can make a burden doubly difficult to bear. I have found that a lot of the answers I sought regarding why we suffer have come to me through the process of maturing spiritually. For example, I have learned that some suffering is actually beneficial to me. Some of it I need to embrace and let it do its intended work in me, and some of it I need to stand against firmly because Satan's intention is to destroy me. In the future, as I continue to grow in God, perhaps I will understand more, but for now, I will share with you what I have learned.

Being thankful for the many blessings in our lives is like a tonic to the suffering soul. The more we focus on our suffering, the more we suffer, but to find things to be thankful for and focus on them is quite helpful. If one believes that God is good, then even in the midst of their worst suffering they have proven that their trust in God is strong and can endure all seasons of life. Our words of gratitude in the face of suffering, especially unjust suffering, are a stronger proof of our trust in God than any other thing I know of.

Suffering is real and it is painful. It is sometimes quite horrific and seemingly unbearable. It may be physical, spiritual, mental, emotional, financial, or relational. Jesus suffered more than any of us ever will, and yet God's Word says that He learned obedience through what He suffered (see Hebrews 5:8). Jesus was never disobedient. He remained thankful and always displayed a loving attitude. But through His suffering, He experienced what obedience to God often costs, and He was willing to pay the price in order to be equipped to serve as the Author and Source of our salvation (see Hebrews 5:9; 12:2). He is the High Priest who understands every pain we experience in this life (see Hebrews 4:15). Jesus never asks us to go where He has not been. It comforts me to know that He has always gone before me and prepared the way that I might walk in it.

> *Jesus never asks us to go where He has not been.*

With those things in mind, let me give you a few things to consider when dealing with the suffering that we face at times in this life.

Sin Is the Root Cause of All Suffering

We have established that our own sin, someone else's sin, or the result of living in a sinful and fallen world is the cause of all suffering, but I would like to unpack this a bit more so we have a better understanding. God's original intention was not for man to experience agony and torment, and it is unfair to blame Him for it.

One of the ways that most of us suffer at some time in our lives is through sickness. When we hear that sin and sickness are often connected, it is easy to become too introspective in trying to locate our sin. Although it is true that something I did may have caused the sickness, that is not always, or even usually, the case.

There is no example in the Bible of Jesus ever connecting a specific sin with a specific sickness or disease. He is our Healer, and He often used healing as a way of convincing people that if He could heal diseases, then surely He could also forgive sin (see Mark 2:9–11). A proper and thorough study of God's Word reveals that healing as well as forgiveness of sin is included in the atonement of Christ (see Isaiah 53:4–5). God simply cannot be our Healer and also be the cause of sickness. Let us settle it once and for all in our hearts that God is good and the devil is bad!

When cold and flu season comes around every year, all kinds of people suffer the effects of these illnesses—good people and evil people, young and old! It is quite random and very doubtful that the ones who catch a cold or the flu are the sinners and those who don't are sinless. However, I think it may be wise when we experience sickness to ask God if we have opened a door in some way for the illness. Quite often we have not acted wisely in how we have taken care of ourselves and it has weakened our immune system, making us more vulnerable to the sickness than we would have been had we behaved differently. Although God may reveal something to us that we should avoid in the future, there are also times when He doesn't. When He is silent, I simply ask for healing and trust God to work good out of it.

This is easy to understand if we talk about a cold or the flu, but it becomes much more difficult when the disease is cancer or some other painful, life-threatening situation. And the more painful the situation, the more difficult it is for us to understand it.

I had breast cancer in 1989, and only recently have I realized that I might have avoided it if I had been wiser in how I cared for my body. At that time in my life, our ministry was fairly new and I lived under constant stress because I didn't yet know much about trusting God and being patient. In addition to trying to develop a ministry, I was walking through an internal healing process with God that was also painful and difficult. I didn't sleep enough, I didn't get proper exercise, I worked too hard, I didn't rest enough, I ate too much junk food, I drank too much coffee, I didn't drink enough water, I was angry and upset very often, I was frustrated—and the list goes on and on. The result was that the stress caused a hormonal imbalance that affected my menstrual cycle, and I ended up going to a doctor, who recommended that I have a hysterectomy and then give myself shots of estrogen. It helped a great deal, and ultimately, I took a shot every ten days. After a year or so, I was diagnosed with an estrogen-dependent breast tumor. In other words, it fed on and grew as a result of estrogen. It was a fast-growing and dangerous type of cancer, and I had to have a radical surgery.

God did not chastise me in this situation or blame me for not taking better care of myself. The surgery was successful and I needed no further treatment. To me that was a miracle in itself. But God did use the situation as an opportunity to begin teaching me the importance of respecting my body since it was His temple, and I now make much better daily decisions regarding my physical health. I have come to the point of personally believing that since we are bought with a price and belong to God, and since our bodies are the temple (the home) of God, it is sinful to disrespect and abuse our bodies. If that thought seems too extreme to you, then set it aside for now, but I urge you to value yourself enough to take good care of yourself.

I have found in talking with people that many—perhaps even most—abuse their bodies. We may simply lack knowledge about the importance of being healthy, and for this reason (if for no other), it is wise to seek God about the true source of any illness we have. I suggest that you invest time reading one good book on how to be healthy in spirit, soul, and body, and I truly believe it will open your eyes to many things that you may previously have been blind to.

God was very merciful and gracious to me when I had cancer, and the outcome could not have been better. I want to be clear that in sharing my experience, I am in no way saying that others who get cancer are not taking care of themselves. I don't know all the reasons behind sickness and disease, but I do know that we should invest in our health and stay as strong as possible. Satan roams the earth looking for someone to seize upon and devour, and I am going to do all I can to make sure it isn't me. 1 Peter 5:8 (AMPC) says, "Be well balanced . . . be vigilant and cautious at all times; for that enemy of yours, the devil, roams around like a lion roaring [in fierce hunger], seeking someone to seize upon and devour." Peter tells us to be well balanced in order to avoid being devoured. I was definitely out of balance in the way I approached life. We cannot break God's laws of health that are found in His

Word and expect to have no ill effects from it. At the very least, we will be tired if we don't take good care of ourselves.

Recently I had a total hip replacement surgery due to arthritis and malformation of the hip joint in my body. Although I was amazed by how good my recovery was, I did experience some days of severe pain caused by excessive activity on my part. The pain was my body's way of telling me to slow down, decrease my activity, and be more patient. My doctor even told me to let pain be my guide in what I could and could not do. He said, "If you do too much one day and have increased pain the next day, then decrease your activity and let the painful area calm down."

As Paul wrote to the Ephesians: "Do all the crisis demands and then stand firmly in your place" (see Ephesians 6:13). Abide in Christ, abide in His love, and trust Him to heal you. Do what God shows you to do and then rest in His love, expecting full restoration and healing.

The Wise Man Suffers Less than the Foolish One

Although the wise man doesn't avoid all suffering, he does avoid many things that the foolish do not. According to God's laws, we reap what we sow (see Galatians 6:7; Matthew 7:1–2; Luke 6:31). That to me is a sobering thought and one that we should remember daily.

If a man has been unfaithful to his wife on several occasions, he may well suffer the loss of the relationship. It is his own fault, and he is reaping what he has sown. If a person spends excessively and emotionally and then ends up being pressured by debt, it is his own fault, for he has sown foolishly and is now reaping the results. The book of Proverbs has many references to how a foolish person's words will cause trouble in his life. Here is one example:

> A [self-confident] fool's lips bring contention, and his mouth invites a beating.
> A [self-confident] fool's mouth is his ruin, and his lips are a snare to himself.
>
> Proverbs 18:6–7 (AMPC)

There are also many Scriptures that teach us how beneficial the words of the wise are. This is just one example:

> There are those who speak rashly, like the piercing of a sword, but the tongue of the wise brings healing.
>
> Proverbs 12:18 (AMPC)

In addition to striving to speak wise words, we can choose wise actions. Proverbs teaches us that wisdom is the most valuable thing we can seek after and operate in. The promises made to the wise are abundant and to be desired: favor, riches, long life, promotion, clarity, and protection, to name a few.

It is obvious that we do not immediately reap, or experience, the effects of every foolish choice we have made, otherwise we would all be in serious trouble. Thankfully, we can receive God's forgiveness and His mercy, but when we persistently sow foolishness, we will reap the results and experience some kind of suffering.

We live in a world built on moral foundations, and there are consequences for immoral behavior. For example, if a person drinks alcohol and drives a car, they may be injured or injure someone else. If someone consistently has a bad temper, they will more than likely end up lonely. If they murder someone, although they certainly can be forgiven, they are likely to spend their life in prison. It might not be a bad idea to begin each day thinking about how all of our words and actions have consequences. It might urge us to make wiser decisions.

The apostle Peter speaks about suffering that we deserve and suffering that we do not deserve. He says it is better to suffer unjustly for doing right than it is to suffer justly for doing wrong (see 1 Peter 2:19–20; 4:15–16).

I can definitely say that the more I study God's Word, learn wisdom from it, and apply it to my life, the less I suffer. The Bible is our instruction book for life! And it can help us think carefully about each decision we make, which is important because every choice carries a consequence. Those who follow God's Word will never have to be victims of their circumstances, because not only can they make decisions that will help them overcome them, but they can learn from them. I was a victim of sexual abuse before I learned God's Word, but now I am free from its effects because I have made choices that are in agreement with God's ways.

We Will Suffer Persecution Because of Our Christian Faith

Paul wrote to Timothy reminding him that anyone who intended to live a godly life would suffer persecution because of their religious stand (see 2 Timothy 3:12). Paul also said that although he had suffered persecutions, God had delivered him out of them all (see 2 Timothy 3:11). I'm very grateful that in the midst of all types of suffering, we have the promise of deliverance and the privilege of trusting God for that deliverance. We may have to be patient and endure hardship for a period of time, but God is faithful, and until He delivers us, He will strengthen us to bear the trouble with a good attitude if we are willing to do so.

Very few of us can say that we have taken a strong stand for the cause of Christ and not experienced some persecution. Often this persecution comes in the form of rejection. My personal experience in this area was quite profound and painful. Upon following the call on my life to teach God's Word, I was asked to leave my church and experienced rejection from family and friends. As humans, we find it very difficult to find unity within diversity. We want everyone to be like us because if they are not, we feel that our thoughts, ideas, and actions are being attacked.

I was stepping out of the normal, accepted role for women, and I believed that I had heard from God. It was enough to send people into an outrage. Who did I think I was? I had no proper education. I was a woman, and women didn't do such things in our religious circles. I didn't realize it at the time, but it was the devil's first attempt to try to get me to give up and stay right where I was, which was miserable and unfulfilling.

The apostles received a warning from the Holy Spirit that they would be persecuted, and yet they boldly went forward. Jesus teaches us that those who hear the Word and "receive it with joy [but accept it only superficially]" endure for a little while, but when persecution (suffering) comes on account of the Word, they are immediately offended and stumble and fall away (see Mark 4:16–17).

We all want to be accepted. No one enjoys the pain of rejection; it is an emotional pain that can be quite intense, and its effects can linger with us for a long time. Jesus was rejected and despised (see Isaiah 53:3). Actually, John 15:25 says He was hated without a cause. He was good and had done nothing wrong and yet He was persecuted. And He tells us that the student is not above his master (see Luke 6:40). If He suffered, we can expect to suffer also.

I want to share a couple of verses about suffering that were difficult for me to grasp in the earlier years of my life:

> For one is regarded favorably (is approved, acceptable, and thankworthy) if, as in the sight of God, he endures the pain of unjust suffering...
>
> For even to this were you called [it is inseparable from your vocation]. For Christ also suffered for you, leaving you [His personal] example, so that you should follow in His footsteps.
>
> 1 Peter 2:19, 21 (AMPC)

I could not understand why God could be pleased when I suffer, but I finally realized it is not my pain and suffering that pleases Him, but the fact that I am willing to do it for His sake. It is not our suffering that glorifies God, but our ability to have a good attitude in suffering. Whenever we suffer, God suffers with us, just as we suffer when our children suffer. There is nothing that can separate us from God's love, and He never leaves us, not for one moment (see Romans 8:38-39; Hebrews 13:5). Even though we may *feel* that He has abandoned us, just as Jesus did on the cross, He has not. Whatever you might be

Whatever you might be going through right now, please know that God is with you and He has a plan for your deliverance and healing.

going through right now, please know that God is with you and He has a plan for your deliverance and healing.

Jesus said we are blessed when we are persecuted for righteousness' sake and that our reward will be great in Heaven (see Matthew 5:10–12). In case you are like me and would prefer not to have to wait until you get to Heaven to see any reward, Jesus also said that if we give up anything for His sake and the Gospel's sake, we will reap in this lifetime and in the age to come (see Mark 10:29–30). From these two Scriptures we see the promise of reward both in Heaven and on earth.

One of the things we often must give up in order to serve God with our whole hearts is our reputation. Jesus made Himself of no reputation (see Philippians 2:7), and it is easy now for me to understand why. If we care too much about what people think of us, we will never fully follow Christ. I sacrificed my reputation with those whom I knew at the time God called me, and now He has rewarded me. I have many more friends now than what I gave up long ago.

God rewards those who diligently seek Him (see Hebrews 11:6). When you are suffering persecution, look forward to the reward that God has planned for you! If you are suffering the loss of your reputation, or being unfairly judged and criticized because of your faith in God, don't despair. Continue trusting God and look forward to your reward.

CHAPTER 11

Reasons Why We Suffer (Part 2)

In the previous chapter, I dealt with three reasons why we suffer. The first one was the existence of sin. Second, I talked about suffering due to not making wise choices. And third, I talked about suffering as a result of being persecuted for our faith in God.

In this chapter I want to continue dealing with reasons why we suffer, and I pray it will be helpful to you in your walk with God.

We Suffer Unjustly Due to Other People's Sins

This type of suffering is very hard for us to endure because we feel we are totally innocent and yet we are suffering for something that is beyond our control. The first thought we have is, *This is not fair*, and it surely is not. But even though life is not always fair, those who put their trust in God can expect to see His justice—in His time and His way. Because God loves justice, He delights in making wrong things right. He is our Vindicator and He compensates us when we are treated unjustly.

Whether it is abuse in childhood, being treated unfairly

because of the color of your skin, your sex, your nationality, or thousands of other things, unjust treatment always hurts deeply, and if we don't deal with it properly, it can leave deep wounds and scars in our soul that affect how we live.

One of God's character traits that I get the most excited about is that He is a God of justice. Here is one of His promises that we can put our trust in:

> For we know Him who said, "Vengeance is Mine [retribution and the deliverance of justice rest with Me], I will repay [the wrongdoer]." And again, "The Lord will judge His people."
>
> Hebrews 10:30

Wow! This is a wonderful and comforting Scripture, and if you are suffering due to unjust treatment from someone else, you should hide this Scripture in your heart and trust God to bring its promise to pass in your life.

I have experienced His justice in my own life on many occasions. I mentioned the rejection I experienced early in my ministry, and even though it took many years, several of the people who hurt me deeply have since apologized and said that the way they treated me was wrong.

To be compensated for an injustice means you are paid back for what has happened to you. There is nothing sweeter than watching God honor and bless you because someone has treated you unfairly. But we have to give up trying to make others pay us back for the injustices we've endured if we want to see God vindicate us.

After being sexually abused by my father and abandoned in the situation by my mother and other relatives who did nothing to help me, I definitely had attitudes that were poisoning my life. I wanted to get back at the people who hurt me, as well as the ones who did not help me. I was bitter, filled with resentment, and felt that the world owed me something. Of course, none of those attitudes were working well for me. They were not solving my problem or making me feel better, but they did continue to make me miserable. I had been abused, which was bad enough, but many years later I was still a victim and stuck in what had happened. I truly felt that I would never have a normal or emotionally healthy life.

I was a Christian, but I didn't really know God's Word. I was born again, but I still did things my way instead of learning and following God's ways. Once I learned that God loved justice and wanted to deal with the things from my past Himself, instead of me trying to do it my way, everything started changing for me. I won't say that it all happened overnight, but gradually my brokenness was healed and God truly took the bad things that were done to me and worked them out for good.

God requires us to let go of the past and forgive our enemies completely, to pray for them and even bless them as He leads us in how to do that. My father eventually apologized to me and wept in repentance. I had the privilege of leading him to the Lord and baptizing him. He told me how proud he was of me and of the work I am blessed to do in ministry.

I think it might be safe to say that most of our suffering in life comes from unjust treatment by evil people, but some of it can come from people who say they love us. When that is the case, the wounds are even deeper. But no matter how deep or intense a problem has been, God can reach it, heal it, work good out of it, and recompense you for past pain.

He gives us beauty for ashes, and joy to replace mourning (see Isaiah 61:1–3). And He promises to pay us back for what we have lost.

> God, your God, will restore everything you lost; he'll have compassion on you; he'll come back and pick up the pieces from all the places where you were scattered.
>
> Deuteronomy 30:3 (MSG)

Nobody wants suffering and pain in their life, but it is good to know that when you are going through it, God is ready to compensate you if you will follow His ways and trust Him to do so.

We Suffer Because We Try to Change Things That Only God Can Change

I think one of the first things I had to learn that alleviated a lot of my emotional suffering was that I was not in control of the universe. Being born with a naturally strong temperament and an aggressive, "take charge" attitude, I struggled due to trying to control and change many things that I had no authority over. It took me several painful years to understand that God was much more interested in changing me than He was in changing my unpleasant circumstances. Of course, I also struggled with trying to change the people in my world so they would make me happier and suit me better, but I had to learn (and it did not come easily or quickly) that only God can change people, and even He won't do it if they don't want His help.

Once I learned to value people where they were instead of where I wanted them to be (and I am still learning it daily), much of my suffering and misery ceased. I was in desperate need of humility, and although God invites us to "humble ourselves," very few of us are willing to do it, so He does it for us. He accomplishes this by putting us in situations with people who frustrate and irritate us, and through our desperation to stop suffering as a result of them, we finally realize that God is using them to get at deep problems in us. He is our deliverer, and although He may take longer than we would like Him to, God will always use the bad things in our lives to work out something good!

Have you considered that your *reaction* to your problem may be the real problem instead of what you initially thought it was? I thought for years that I was unhappy because Dave wasn't meeting my needs, but God showed me that my selfish attitude was the real problem. I kept trying to change him, and none of my efforts produced the desired result, because God was using the situation to get to the real root of my problem.

The Word of God tells us that a little shepherd boy, David, was anointed to be king. But long before he wore the crown, he had to work under and deal with the mad and evil king he was destined to replace. So much of what happened to David at the hands of Saul seemed unfair, and yet there was a purpose in it.

I heard once that God used King Saul to get the "Saul" out of David before he became a king just like him. I know that to be true in my own life. I can look back at the cruelty that was in my father's behavior, and I now recognize that I learned a lot of his traits, but I didn't realize it at the time. I was a woman who was called into ministry, but I was hard-hearted from the abuse I had suffered as a child. My ways were harsh, and I was very legalistic regarding what I thought people should and should not do. A relationship with me meant following my rules, and I stress "my" rules! I had charisma, but was lacking in the Christian character needed for the job in front of me. I was blind to my behavior because it was rooted in the wounds and bruises in my soul that needed to be dealt with. Being a Christian does not mean that we spend our lives in behavior modification, but we do need to let Jesus transform us from the inside out and mold us into His image.

God used a spiritual leader, and a few other people who did not treat me well, to help me realize that I should never treat others the way they had treated me. God actually did me a favor by putting me in close contact with these people for a number of years, and although it was very painful, it helped me tremendously and made me a better person. I like to say that sometimes we need something difficult or uncomfortable to happen to help us see ourselves as we truly are instead of the way we think we are. Our thinking can easily be clouded with pride, causing us to critically judge others, and even though we may do some of the same things we criticize them for, we don't see it (see Romans 2:1).

I find Peter to be a good example in this area. Peter was aggressive and always had plenty to say. He was destined for great things, but he thought more highly of himself than he should have. His attitude needed to be dealt with for his own benefit. When Jesus told him that Satan was going to sift him like wheat in the upcoming trials they would go through but that He had prayed for him that his faith wouldn't fail, Peter quickly declared that he was ready to go to prison and even to die with Jesus if he needed to. He ended up denying Christ three times that day, and because of his failure, he finally saw himself as he truly was. He was a weak man who needed forgiveness and God's help. (See Luke 22:31–34, 55–62.) When Jesus told Peter that He had prayed for him, Peter should have thanked Him and admitted that he desperately needed all the help he could get.

After denying Christ, Peter repented and wept bitterly, and he went on to become one of the greatest and most effective apostles. It is not our weaknesses that cause us problems, but our unwillingness to deal with them. We would be wise to ask God daily to help us and to show us anything about ourselves that is hindering Him from doing as He pleases with us. We should always want God's will more than we want anything else.

Peter exhorts us to humble ourselves under the mighty hand of God that in due time He may exalt us (see 1 Peter 5:6). To humble oneself is to stay under a thing rather than struggle to get free of it because it is difficult. None of us want to suffer, but we should be willing to do so if it is required of us.

Let's suppose a woman is married to a man who physically abuses her and their children. In that situation, she should definitely not stay under the abuse. She should get away from the man. My mother stayed with my father, knowing what he was doing to me, and it was possibly the worst mistake she made in her entire life.

But let's say that a person works at a company where she is the only Christian and therefore the only one in a position to witness for Christ. She is rejected and made fun of by many of the other workers and even passed over for promotions she deserves. Does she leave because it is uncomfortable for her, or does she pray that if God wants her to leave, He will make that clear, and if He doesn't then His will be done? In this instance, God may want her to stay under the difficulty for a season because He needs an instrument there that He can use to represent Him. 2 Timothy 4:2 says we should be ready to serve God "whether the opportunity seems favorable or unfavorable, whether convenient or inconvenient, whether welcome or unwelcome."

When a situation or person is causing us to suffer, we should always seek God about how we should handle it. It is not wise to make decisions while we are hurting without consulting the Holy Spirit for guidance. Paul told the Galatians that if they were spiritual, they would bear (put up with) one another's troublesome faults (see Galatians 6:2). My first inclination would be to say, "I don't have to put up with this and I'm not going to," but on the other hand, Jesus puts up with me and I am glad He does.

I have realized after going through many different things in my life that God will always give us grace for our place. In other words, if we are where

> God will always give us grace for our place.

He wants us to be, then He can give enough grace for us to actually enjoy what might make others miserable.

When I look back at the early years of my walk with God, it seems that I was struggling with something all the time. If it wasn't one thing then it was another. My mood was almost totally controlled by my circumstances. For example, when one of my conferences was well attended, I had joy, but when it wasn't well attended, I became discouraged and said a lot of negative things. So we would do everything possible to increase the attendance, but when it was still up and down, then I went up and down with it. I finally realized I was trying to change something that I could not change, but that God could, and He would, when the time was right. Truly our times are in His hands (see Psalm 31:15). I eventually gave my concerns to God, and sure enough, peace came just as He promised it would (see Philippians 4:6–7).

Our conferences are attended a lot better now, but occasionally we still have one that isn't for some reason, and although I still don't like it, it doesn't cause me to suffer as it once did, simply because I don't fight it. I go through it and go on to the next one.

The next time you find yourself suffering emotionally and mentally because you're trying to change something that you don't like, ask yourself if you're trying to do something that only God can do, and if you are, then I urge you to "let go and let God."

We Suffer Because We Live in an Imperfect World

We have seen that we can suffer due to personal sin, or the sin of other people, but one of the major reasons why we suffer is simply because we live in the world—a world filled with sin—and it seems the longer the earth remains, the more evil is compounded. I think in every generation people have been shocked at how bad things have gotten in the world. I remember when I was a child hearing adults talk about how bad things were, and now we talk about how shocked we are at what is going on in the world, and unless the Lord returns first, our children will someday sit around and talk about how much worse things are in their generation than they have ever been. Evil and wickedness are progressive. They don't remain static, but they compound and multiply. Dave remembers when the first newspaper boy was robbed in our city, and that was about 1950. It was shocking to people and they just couldn't fathom something like that happening. But if we look at what is happening today, a newspaper boy being robbed wouldn't raise any eyebrows or shock us at all. It is troubling that conditions are as bad as they are, and, sadly, the worse things become the more suffering there will be. Although we don't have all the answers, we do have the privilege of trusting God.

Does God protect those who put their trust in Him? I definitely believe that He does. We often hear stories of how God protected someone, and we have stories of our own. But what about the times when His protection doesn't seem to be there and we end up suffering something that we just don't understand? Let's go back again to the wise comment that I heard from Lee Strobel:

"God's ultimate answer to suffering isn't an explanation; it's the incarnation." Nobody can explain it all, but Jesus can redeem it all.

One of our employees recently lost her home and all of its contents in a flood we had in St. Louis. She is the head of our medical missions and has sacrificed a great deal to travel to third world countries and help people. She is a godly woman and comes from a godly family. Why would this happen to her? Sometimes painful things happen just because we are in the world. The good news is that God is redeeming her entire situation. People and various ministries are helping her family to rebuild and purchase what they need, and by the time it is all over, she may have a better house and furniture than she had before.

I know other Christians who came close to losing their homes and didn't. They feel that God protected them, and when we hear their testimonies, we rejoice with them. Why were some spared and others were not? Once again, we should not focus on finding an explanation; let's turn to the incarnation and watch God redeem and restore the pain and turn it into gain.

CHAPTER 12

On the Other Side of Suffering

His feet they hurt with fetters; he was laid in chain of iron and his soul entered into the iron.

Psalm 105:18 (AMPC)

Joseph was a young man with a dream of doing great things. His brothers hated him and were jealous of him because he was the youngest son of Jacob and was favored. Their hatred became so intense that they took him out one day and sold him to slave traders, and then they brought back a blood-soaked piece of clothing and lied to their father, saying that he had been killed by a wild animal.

Joseph went through many years of tragic, unfair situations that caused him a great deal of suffering, and yet he remained faithful to God and continued to trust Him. God gave him favor wherever he was and eventually positioned him as second in command under the pharaoh of Egypt. As a result, God used Joseph to save many people—including his own family—from starvation during a severe famine in the land. It's amazing to see Joseph's response to his brothers when they discovered that he was in a position of power and could pay them back for all the pain and suffering he had unjustly endured because of their cruel treatment of him all those years ago:

Then his brothers went and fell down before him, saying,
See, we are your servants (your slaves)!

And Joseph said to them, Fear not; for am I in the place
of God? [Vengeance is His, not mine.]

As for you, you thought evil against me, but God meant
it for good, to bring about that many people should be
kept alive, as they are this day.

Genesis 50:18–20 (AMPC)

These Scriptures are quite wonderful if we ponder them carefully. After all Joseph had been through, instead of being bitter,
he saw God's hand working good out of the entire situation. Now,
rather than be bitter, he was prepared to help his brothers. This is
the rest of what he said:

Now therefore, do not be afraid. I will provide for and support
you and your little ones. And he comforted them [imparting
cheer, hope, strength] and spoke to their hearts [kindly].

Genesis 50:21 (AMPC)

Joseph is my hero when it comes to someone who experienced
tragic, unjust treatment and handled it exactly the way God
wants us to. No wonder he was a powerful man. He lived to be
110 years old and appears to have enjoyed many more good years
in his life than the ones that he suffered through. Joseph enjoyed
great victory on the other side of his suffering. We might say that
his suffering promoted him to a better life. If we can remain sta-
ble and continue trusting God, even in our suffering, then we
show ourselves to be the kind of people that God can trust with
great responsibility and great blessings.

When we are willing to forgive those who have hurt us, we are actually doing ourselves a favor, because it is impossible to enjoy life and be filled with bitterness at the same time. This example we see from the life of Joseph is one that we should follow.

> *When we are willing to forgive those who have hurt us, we are actually doing ourselves a favor.*

During the years after Joseph was sold into slavery, he went to prison for thirteen years for something he was not guilty of. He was in chains of iron, and in Psalm 105, which I quoted earlier, we are told that "his soul entered into the iron." What does that mean? If we think about it on a practical level, it would seem to me that if his soul entered into the iron, it made him stronger. In other words, his suffering actually made him a better person and helped equip him to rule over Egypt.

We often hear the phrase "Our troubles can make us better or bitter," and it is very true. Trusting God all the way through painful situations always carries with it a reward and pays dividends in the end. One of the rewards is that it makes you stronger.

In the book of Isaiah, we see God speaking through the prophet to the people and encouraging them not to fear what they were going through because He was making them stronger:

> Fear not [there is nothing to fear], for I am with you; do not look around you in terror and be dismayed, for I am your God. I will strengthen and harden you to difficulties, yes, I will help you; I will hold you up and retain you with My [victorious] right hand of rightness and justice...

> Behold, I will make you to be a new, sharp, threshing instrument which has teeth; you shall thresh the mountains and beat them small, and shall make the hills like chaff.
>
> Isaiah 41:10, 15 (AMPC)

This is another example of God's promise to use what we go through to make us stronger and better than we were before. But this all hinges on whether or not we are willing to put our total trust in God concerning the painful things we encounter in life. Whatever you might be going through right now, this promise is for you. Your enemies may mean harm, but God will work it out for good, and in the process, He will make you a better person. When life is painful and hard, remember that God loves you, and because of that you don't have to be afraid. Here is a short story I once heard that makes this point in a cute way:

A man had just gotten married and was returning home with his wife. Part of their journey required that they cross a lake in a boat. While they were doing so, a storm arose that caused the boat to toss about vehemently, and the woman became afraid. Her husband, however, seemed very calm, and she kept asking why he wasn't afraid.

He smiled and withdrew a knife from its holder, and held it close to the woman as if he was going to harm her. She didn't even flinch, and when he asked her why she wasn't afraid, she said, "Why should I be afraid? I know that you love me, and it would be impossible for you to hurt me."

The man said, "That is why I am not afraid in this storm. I know that God loves us, and that no matter what happens, He will work it out for our good."

No matter how many storms we encounter in life, we are always safe in God's loving hands.

Compassion and Empathy

I have found that my own suffering in life helped me gain much greater compassion for those who are also suffering in some way. If we have not experienced the pain of being mistreated or encountered loss, it is very difficult to relate to what others are going through.

It is easy to give advice, but without some experience, our attitudes may be a bit dismissive. Let's pretend that I am twenty-five years old and life for me has been pretty easy up to this point. I had great parents who always provided for me and gave me most of what I wanted. I am intelligent, so getting good grades came easy for me in college. My father secured a dream job for me from one of his business associates even before I graduated from school. Life is good! Now an associate at work whom I've gotten to know quite well seems to be discouraged and even depressed and I wonder what is wrong, but I don't bother to ask. Eventually my friend tries to tell me about some serious financial struggles that she is having. I quickly suggest that she call her parents and ask them to help her, because that would be what I would do. She informs me that her parents were abusive to her as she grew up and that they are estranged. She assures me that getting help from them is not even possible. Since I cannot even imagine parents abusing their children, or not helping them, I dismiss her problem with an insensitive statement. I say, "Don't worry, something will work out," and I walk away.

My friend is left feeling empty and lonely. The really sad part is that I am so blessed financially because of the generosity of my parents that I could easily have given her some help myself, but my lack of experience with suffering has left me unsympathetic toward those who are hurting.

There are lots of people like this in the world. They are not bad people, but they are inexperienced. They will eventually encounter some difficulty in life that, hopefully, will change them for the better.

I am not like the twenty-five-year-old who had an easy life. I never had parents who really loved or helped me in any way while I was growing up, and they were abusive. My childhood was filled with fear, suffering, and loneliness. I would like to say that I came out of my childhood with a lot of compassion for those who are suffering, but instead I only had a hard heart. It took a deep relationship with Christ, and several years of gaining more experience through personal pain and suffering, before I changed.

When I had cancer, I gained a lot more compassion for those who receive such a serious diagnosis. After having migraine headaches for ten years, I have faith now to pray compassionately for the healing of people with headaches. Through the grace of God and His Word, I was finally able to forgive my father for sexually abusing me, and I know firsthand how much better it is to forgive than to be filled with hatred and bitterness. I began a ministry with nothing but God and a dream, and I am still at it forty years later. I have learned a lot by experience, but it has been costly. I experienced many people who judged and criticized me and felt that I was unfit for the ministry for many different reasons, but I also experienced the comfort of God in those situations, and I am now able to comfort others. God teaches us the grace of bringing comfort to those who are suffering by comforting us Himself when we are suffering.

Blessed be the God and Father of our Lord Jesus Christ,
the Father of sympathy (pity and mercy) and the God

[Who is the Source] of every comfort (consolation and
encouragement),

Who comforts (consoles and encourages) us in every
trouble (calamity and affliction), so that we may also
be able to comfort (console and encourage) those who
are in any kind of trouble or distress, with the comfort
(consolation and encouragement) with which we ourselves
are comforted (consoled and encouraged) by God.

2 Corinthians 1:3–4 (AMPC)

I vividly recall how often I tried to share with other people
what I was going through, and they simply did not know how to
help me. They could not relate to my pain because they had none
of their own. They could not comfort me because they had never
needed God to comfort them, or perhaps they needed it but did
not know how to ask for and receive it. I often say that we cannot
give away what we do not have. First we must receive from God,
and then what He has given us can flow through us to others.

When people come to us with their problems, most of the time
they already know that we cannot solve them. What they really
want is understanding, comfort, and compassion. On the other
side of suffering, we can become softer, more tender, gentler, and
more compassionate and empathetic. These qualities are some of
what we admire in our Lord and they qualify us to minister on
His behalf.

Developing compassion and empathy for others is one of the
blessings we end up with on the other side of suffering. The simple gift of compassion is very valuable to someone who is hurting!

It is not our suffering alone that qualifies us to be used by God
to help others. Certainly, God can and does use people mightily
who had great parents, a good childhood, no financial struggles,

and every other advantage. However, there are very few such people, simply because life happens to us all, and it is not always kind.

A Deeper Relationship with God

One of the benefits I have found on the other side of suffering is a deeper relationship with God. When we are put in a position where we have no one who can help us except God and we put our trust in Him, we experience the many wonders of who He is and how good He is. We experience His faithfulness, His justice, kindness, mercy, grace, wisdom, and power, to name just a few. Paul said that his determined purpose was to know Christ and to become more deeply and intimately acquainted with the wonders of His Person. He said that he wanted to know the power of Christ's resurrection, and then he said, "[that I may share] the fellowship of His sufferings" (see Philippians 3:10).

There are several powerful points in this Scripture:

1. Paul was determined!

Determination is required if we want to accomplish anything in life. It is not what we do right once or twice that brings victory, but what we do right repeatedly that gets us the desired result.

2. Paul wanted to know Christ more deeply and intimately.

He did not merely want to know *about* Him, he wanted to *know Him*! He wanted to have an intimate, personal relationship with

Him. This is available to anyone who desires it and is willing to seek Jesus wholeheartedly.

3. Paul wanted to know the wonders of Christ's Person more strongly and clearly.

Paul knew Christ. He had an amazing encounter with Him on the Damascus Road, and yet he was searching for more. We should never be satisfied if we are not growing spiritually. There is so much more to learn about how amazing Jesus is, and we will know more if we seek Him more. As we make our journey in life with Him, we find that He is with us in all kinds of situations. He never leaves us or forsakes us.

4. Paul wanted to experience the power of Christ's resurrection that lifts us out from among the dead even while still in the body.

When we truly know Jesus deeply and intimately, we can have peace and joy even during difficult times. We trust Him to work good things out of whatever we are dealing with no matter how painful it is. We don't have to live a defeated life when Jesus' resurrection power is available.

When we have experienced God's power in our lives, it becomes easier to trust Him the next time we have a need. God wants to show His power in us and through us. He not only wants to deliver us, but He wants to use us as ambassadors to draw people to Christ.

If you or I are going through some serious difficulty and other people see that we continue to trust God and maintain a peaceful and joyful attitude, it witnesses to them about the keeping power of God. When we wait patiently, no matter how long it takes, it witnesses to them about the stabilizing power of God. Then, when we experience deliverance and they see that God is faithful, it witnesses to them of His presence and

> *Our personal example may be the tipping point that causes a person to surrender his life to Christ.*

power, as well as His desire to help us. Our personal example may be the tipping point that causes a person to surrender his life to Christ.

5. *Paul said that he was willing to share the sufferings of Christ if that would cause him to be transformed into the image of Christ.*

That doesn't mean that we need to hang on a cross as Jesus did. It simply means that we should be willing to go through whatever we need to in order to be like Jesus and see Him glorified through us.

Does this mean that God gives us suffering and trials in order for us to learn things that will benefit us later? He is not a God who takes His children out behind the woodshed to give them a thrashing in order to teach them.

I prefer to say that once we have a problem or difficulty, God may well use it to further His purpose in our lives. If we are going to suffer, why not get some benefit from it? I have suffered without

> *If we are going to suffer, why not get some benefit from it?*

God in my life, and I have suffered with Him, and I can firmly say that *with God* is always better. I believe that God always has a plan for our deliverance, but He may delay it for a time in order to use it for our growth and character development. His timing is perfect in our lives, and while we are waiting, we have the privilege of trusting Him.

For the Joy of Obtaining the Prize

Jesus said that even though He despised the shame of the cross, He endured it for the joy of obtaining the prize on the other side of it (see Hebrews 12:2). Numerous people have told me that they wouldn't trade what they went through for anything, simply because of how it changed them and brought them closer to God.

We may despise what we are going through while we are going through it. No one enjoys any kind of pain or suffering. But if we can set our minds on the prize, on the other side, we will be able to endure it more joyfully. If we continue having faith that we will see the goodness of God no matter how badly we hurt or how long it takes, we will taste the sweetness of breakthrough and victory.

I often say that we have to "go through" to "get through." Don't be afraid of difficulty, because God will not give you more than you can han-

> *We have to "go through" to "get through."*

dle with Him in your life helping and guiding you.

CHAPTER 13

Day by Day

Then the Lord said to Moses, Behold, I will rain bread from the heavens for you; and the people shall go out and gather a day's portion every day...

Exodus 16:4 (AMPC)

When God gave the Israelites the bread from Heaven, it wasn't only to feed them but to test their trust in Him. He commanded them to take only what they needed for the day and trust that when tomorrow came, He would also provide for that day. Just imagine how difficult that may have been for many of them. They were in a wilderness and had no food and no way of getting any. I am sure their fear was quite high. I know mine would have been!

There are going to be times when God tests us in areas to see if we will trust Him or not. If the Israelites did try to gather tomorrow's portion today, it rotted and began to stink. How often do we try to gather today what we need for tomorrow through reasoning or worry and all it does is make us miserable?

Recently I woke up in the morning and promptly began thinking about all of the writing projects I had that were coming due around the same time. In addition, I had a conference coming up that I needed to prepare for, some television to do, a couple of business meetings, and several personal appointments! The more I thought about all I had to do over the next thirty days or so, the more pressured and overloaded I felt. God simply spoke to my heart, reminding me of something I already knew: *Live one day at a time*. Immediately I felt the pressure lift, because I have enough experience with God to know beyond a doubt that He will enable us to do everything He wants us to do if we take it one day at a time.

When we use today to worry about tomorrow, we end up wasting today. It is useless! Jesus said not to worry about tomorrow because tomorrow would have sufficient trouble of its own (see Matthew 6:34). God helps us as we put our trust in Him, not as we worry and fret about how we are going to solve our problems.

In 2013 we released a daily devotional titled *Trusting God Day by Day*, and it has been one of our most popular devotionals. Why? It is popular because it presents something we feel we can do. Looking at all of life at once, or even one week or a month, is usually overwhelming, but one day at a time is doable. Alcoholics Anonymous uses this principle with the men and women who come to them for help. People often feel that there is no way they can go the rest of their life without a drink; the fear of failure is so strong that they don't even want to begin. But the thought of not drinking one day at a time seems to be a possibility. Their goal is to stay sober for one day, and many of them can tell you exactly how many days they have been sober even if years have gone by since they had their last drink.

Because this principle comes straight out of God's Word, it works in most areas of life. We can get out of debt, exercise, lose weight, graduate from college, parent a special needs child, or be successful at anything we need to do if we will put our trust in God and take life one day at a time.

I love this quote by an unknown source: "I try to take life one day at a time, but sometimes several days attack me at once."

The Difference Between Faith and Trust

The words "faith" and "trust" are often used interchangeably, but is there a difference? In many ways the two are similar, because both require confidence in God, but "faith" is a noun and therefore it is something we have, while "trust" is often used as a verb and is something that we do.

God gives us faith. His Word says that

> Trust is faith in action.

every man is given a measure of faith (see Romans 12:3), but it is up to the individual what they do with it. Trust is faith in action. It is faith that has been released. Just think about all the things people put their faith in other than God—financial systems of the world, the government, education, other people, retirement funds, themselves, and so on. Out of all the things people put their trust in, God is the only source that is completely reliable.

I want you to pay attention to the phrase I am using: "Put your trust in God." "Put" is an action word; when we put anything anywhere, it is based on a decision to do so. I can put this computer back on the charger when I am finished so it will be fully charged and ready to go the next time I use it, or I can leave it lying open on the couch, and the next time I need it, I will find it drained of power and useless to me. I may take a chance that it won't run out of power, but if it does, I end up disappointed. This is similar to what we do when we put our trust in anything or anyone other than God. We take a chance that things will work out well, but our experience teaches us that it doesn't always happen.

Obviously there are things and people we can trust, but there is no guarantee we'll always be satisfied with the outcome. I can truly say that after walking with God for three-quarters of my life, I am completely satisfied with the outcome of putting my trust in Him. Although things didn't always work out the way I thought they would, or the way I wanted them to, I realize now that God always did what was best.

If you have not been doing so, will you make a decision to begin putting your trust in God in every situation in your life? Think about it on a day-by-day basis and it will seem easier to do. Can you trust God for today? Will you put your trust in God for today? Whatever challenging situation you are facing today, will you release it to God and put your trust in Him?

The Bible is filled with Scriptures about people who said they would "put" their trust in God. It was a decision they made. The writers often use the phrase "I will" when speaking about putting their trust in God. Making the decision is the first part, and then we follow through, even just one hour at a time if that is what it takes. Tiny goals eventually help us reach huge ones.

The Bible says:

> O Lord my God, in You I take refuge and *put* my trust; save me from all those who pursue and persecute me, and deliver me.
>
> Psalm 7:1 (AMPC, emphasis mine)

> What time I am afraid, I will have confidence in and *put* my trust and reliance in You.
>
> By [the help of] God I will praise His word; on God I lean, rely, and confidently *put* my trust; I will not fear. What can man, who is flesh, do to me?
>
> Psalm 56:3–4 (AMPC, emphasis mine)

Putting your trust in God will be easier on days when life is going well, but on the days when things aren't going so well, it will be more difficult. If you are facing something really tragic or painful, it will also be difficult, but we should remember that God never tells us to do something that we cannot do. We can trust God day by day! Even if you have days when you must say one thousand times, "I will put my trust in God," it is worth doing. Not only does it honor God, but it lifts burdens off of us that we were neither equipped nor meant to carry.

When I was diagnosed with breast cancer in 1989, it was frightening, and my first impulse was to worry. My mind was filled with "what ifs," but God asked me to say, "God, I trust You," instead of speaking about my fears and worries. Some days I had to say it over and over, but I persisted. Finally the day for surgery came, with the testing of my lymph nodes to see if the cancer had spread, and that meant putting more trust in God each day as we waited for the results of the tests. It seemed like it took a long time, but day by day I continued saying, "God, I trust You." Finally, the report came back and it was good. There was no cancer in the lymph nodes, but the doctors were not sure if any other treatment would be needed. Only the oncologist could tell me that. I made an appointment with the oncologist, but of course it took awhile to get in to see her, so I was facing more days of trusting God before I would know what my life would look like in the next few months. We all know the difficulty of wanting answers and having to wait for them.

During those waiting times, I had plenty of opportunity to let my mind drift to the worst possible scenario, but then God would remind me to trust Him. When I finally saw the oncologist, she said she saw no need for any further treatment since the cancer was completely removed. I could go on with life as normal and just get a checkup every year. What a relief! I felt like I had dropped a five-hundred-pound weight. Then each year for many years, when mammogram time came, I had to go through the process all over again. One year the radiologist thought he saw something on the scan and they wanted me to stay for an ultrasound, and I had to wait a while for that! *What if the cancer has come back? What if it has spread to other places?* These questions and many others had time to rush through my mind while I was waiting, but I said, "Lord, I trust You no matter how this turns out."

I had the ultrasound and it turned out to be absolutely nothing! Once again I was declared cancer-free, and that has continued for twenty-seven years now.

I tell you this story for the purpose of letting you know that I realize that putting your trust in God often requires that you fight the good fight of faith, as Paul told Timothy to do in 1 Timothy 6:12. The devil is a liar, and he definitely tries to take advantage of every situation that he can to fill us with fear, but we can disrupt his plan by willingly choosing to "put" our trust in God!

As you read this, you may feel that you have trusted God in the past and things have not turned out the way you wanted them to. If so, that is not surprising, because things don't always end up being the way we desire them to be. Trusting God—or I should say totally trusting in God—is not about us getting what we want. When we decide to trust God, we're making a total commitment to trust Him no matter the outcome. We give Him the honor of trusting that He knows best.

We can hear that total trust in Job's statement when he said, "Even though He slay me, yet will I trust Him" (see Job 13:15). Job knew that his Redeemer lived and that in the end He would stand on the earth (see Job 19:25). The confident faith and trust that Job displayed in God is the most important message in the book of Job. We often focus so much on why he suffered that we lose sight of the other lessons in the book. Job's faith amazes me, and I find that these Scriptures challenge and empower me to trust God no matter what I am going through.

Job did complain, and he didn't think he deserved the suffering he was enduring, but he never stopped trusting God. In the end, God restored double all that Job had lost, and I imagine that was an awesome feeling. I firmly believe that God rewards those who continue to put their trust in Him.

Very few, if any, of us can go through something tragic without complaining a little, and we probably don't think we deserve our troubles any more than Job did. But in the midst of it all, we can choose to trust God one day at time, and if we will, then we can make it through anything.

What Will My Future Look Like?

We all think we would love to know the future. People spend millions of dollars on fortune-tellers and psychics, hoping to get some information about their future. God's Word condemns such practices, and it is interesting that people spend so much money on these types of things. When we trust God, we have no need to do things like that, because we know He will reveal our future in His own timing, and until He does, we trust Him.

Abraham Lincoln said, "The best thing about the future is that it comes one day at a time."[9] Would we really want to know our future? I think once we did know, we might wish we had never asked. Every life is filled with good things as well as some things that are not good. If we saw the future, we might be excited about part of it, but that enthusiasm would wane as we saw all the things that would be difficult, painful, disappointing, or challenging.

The fact that we face the difficult days one at a time enables us to do so without giving up. We can do anything one day at a time as long as we put our trust in God, leaning and relying on Him. Excessive thinking about our problems causes us to faint in our minds and want to quit on life. If we knew the future, we might be tempted to think and worry about all the hard things we saw in it, and we would more than likely be overwhelmed. I feel quite certain that if God wanted us to know the future, He surely would have made arrangements for us to do so. Anything He hides from us is for a good cause, and we can rest in knowing that He will reveal to us what we need to know at the right time.

At times we are all abased and at other times we abound, and Paul encourages us to be content in both (see Philippians 4:11–12). God uses both in our lives. Not all seasons are the same, but as they work together, they make a beautiful life. When we endure a long winter season, it eventually gives way to spring, and the flowers bloom once more in our lives.

I don't know everything my future holds, but I trust it will be awesome, and I believe yours will be too. Let's take life one day at a time and enjoy the victory that God gives us through trusting Him with all of our heart and mind. Please don't make the mistake of wasting today being worried about tomorrow! God has you in His hands, you are on His mind, and you can do whatever you need to do through Him, who is your strength (see Philippians 4:13).

CHAPTER 14

The Unknown

Who among you fears the Lord and obeys the word of his servant? Let the one who walks in the dark, who has no light, trust in the name of the Lord and rely on their God.

Isaiah 50:10 (NIV)

It is one thing to trust God when we think we have a fairly good idea of what is happening in our lives, or when we think we have things all figured out and a plan in place that will open the door for us to get what we want. However, it is another thing entirely when we have no light regarding our circumstances or future.

Charles Spurgeon said, "To trust God in the light is nothing, but to trust Him in the dark—that is faith."[10] Man has an almost unquenchable desire to know things. He wants to be well informed because he believes it gives him a measure of control over his life. But when we enter into a relationship with God, we are to relinquish control and trust Him to direct our path. Most of us won't do that without some help from God, so He helps us! He allows us to get into situations that we cannot figure out, and He chooses not to give us the answers when we would like them. Life is filled with many mysteries, and our choices on how to handle them are limited. We may frustrate and confuse ourselves trying to gain understanding regarding things that are hidden in the knowledge of God alone, or we can search the minds of other people, asking for their insight on what is taking place in our lives. While that may help sometimes, it may also increase our confusion. The quickest path to peace is to learn to trust God. I believe that trusting God is one of the ways that we show honor

> *The quickest path to peace is to learn to trust God.*

to Him. It shows respect, and declares that we believe His Word and trust His character.

The spirit of fear is the root of our insatiable desire to have all the answers to life. We want to know what is coming up next and exactly how things will turn out for us in the future. We don't want any surprises, at least none that are not completely joyous.

Although there are many things that God does give us insight into, He does not do so all the time, and when He doesn't, we have trust as our "go-to" fail-safe. When we trust God and we are willing to be patient, we will see that He never fails us.

I realize that not knowing is rather disconcerting and causes stress. Our minds flit from one thing to another, trying to find anything that makes sense, but oddly enough, even when we do think we have things all figured out, we may still be wrong. We like everything tucked away in a nice little space in our lives, but there are times when our lives are messy rather than tidy. Nobody, including God, is doing what we want, and all we feel is frustration. At numerous times in my life, I have based my expectations on what I *thought* was going to take place, and then been distraught when it didn't turn out that way.

These types of situations can be used as our pathway to learning, but in order for that to happen, we must calm down and ask God to show us where we went wrong in our thinking. For me, I usually find that I made plans according to what *I* wanted to see take place, instead of even considering what God might want.

The most basic step of faith we can take regarding our situations in life is saying, "Lord, this is what I would like to see happen, but may Your will be done and not mine!"

In the early days of my ministry, I chose a group of friends whom I thought would work with me and help in the birthing of the things God had revealed to me that I would do as a teacher of His Word. Please notice that I said that *I* chose them. I did so without prayer or even acknowledging God in my ways. When Jesus chose His disciples (the men who were to work with Him), He prayed all night before making those choices (see Luke 6:12–13).

The people I chose were not God's choice, and it turned out to be a disaster that caused me a great deal of personal emotional pain. They gossiped about me, lied, made false accusations, and nearly derailed me before I got much of a start in pursuing my destiny.

The choices we make regarding who we will associate with are important, especially if we are to be yoked with them in a close and personal way. Satan often uses people, even Christians, to wound and weaken us. People may be sincere and yet be sincerely wrong. This group of people thought they were hearing things from God about me that absolutely were not true, and their pride ultimately became their downfall.

> *Prayer should precede every important decision that we make.*

Through many such situations in life, I learned the hard way that prayer should precede every important decision that we make. Our presumption and assumption are not pleasing to God! Don't make the mistake of planning and then praying that God will make your plans work. Pray first and let the Holy Spirit guide you into all of God's good will for your life.

Satisfied Not to Know

The apostle Paul was a highly educated man and yet he came to a place in his life where he said, "For I determined not to know anything among you except Jesus Christ and Him crucified" (1 Corinthians 2:2 [NKJV]). In presenting the Gospel to people, he told them that salvation through Christ was a mystery and a secret of God, but that he had chosen to believe it instead of trying to understand it. There are countless people who refuse to enjoy the benefits of simple, childlike faith. They want to mentally understand all the intricacies of the cross of Christ and salvation through Him, but it can only be understood with the heart, not the mind.

If we have no unanswered questions in our lives, then there is no need for faith. We might say that faith often takes the place of answers! We should seek to know the Word, to know God, and to know His will instead of endlessly seeking to know all the answers regarding our circumstances. When people ask what we are going to do when we encounter a problem, we can simply say, "I don't know." Tell people you are praying about everything and that you are assured in your heart that God will give you direction at just the right time. Even if you sound a bit more confident than you actually are, it is still good to voice your faith. If we choose to trust God, our feelings will eventually catch up with our decision.

There is certainly nothing wrong with seeking answers to the mysteries in our lives, but when we become confused or frustrated, that is a sign that we have gone too far in our quest.

People experience a lot of confusion in life, and I believe most of it comes from an out-of-balance need to know everything. Can you have faith in God while you are in the dark and have no understanding concerning your current situation? That is the kind of faith that God is looking for. He wants us to trust Him, especially when we are in the dark, or when life is a mystery and we don't see Him working or feel His presence. These times are actually good for us because they help us grow in faith. The Bible speaks of little faith and great faith, so why should we be satisfied with little faith when we can develop great faith through trusting God in difficult times?

"Need to Know"

I was watching a movie recently that involved two FBI agents with different levels of clearance. One seemed to be privy to information about a case that the other one wasn't aware of, and when he asked for information, he was told that it was given on a "need to know" basis. In other words, the only people being informed of the details in the case were those who really needed to know.

I think God operates with us on that basis also. If we need to know something, we can always be assured that He will tell us, but if we don't need to know, or it is better for us not to know, then He won't tell us, and we can, and should, learn to be satisfied with that.

The knowledge of some things can burden our souls and cause us to worry and be anxious, and none of us need that. In those times, not knowing can be very peaceful! I was talking on the phone with someone last week and a certain distasteful subject came up regarding immorality in the life of a person we both know. We were talking, but also being careful not to gossip or say things that were unnecessary. My friend asked me a question about the situation, and before I could even consider whether or not to answer, she said, "Never mind, I don't need to know that."

I thought that showed spiritual maturity, and it can be an example to all of us. There is a difference between wanting to know something out of curiosity or wanting to control situations, and wanting to know because we truly need to know. Instead of getting confused and frustrated while trying to reason and question things in life, why not simply trust God to work with us on a "need to know" basis?

There are situations in the Bible where man is told to reason with God, but those do not refer to trying to find out things that God is not yet ready to reveal. Here are two scriptural examples that show the difference between reasoning in the will of God and out of the will of God.

> Come now, and let us reason together, says the Lord. Though your sins are like scarlet, they shall be as white as snow; though they are red like crimson, they will be like wool.
>
> Isaiah 1:18 (AMPC)

> Lean on, trust in, and be confident in the Lord with all your heart and mind and do not rely on your own insight or understanding.
>
> Proverbs 3:5 (AMPC)

Once again, I want to be clear that it is not wrong to ask God questions. He often likes to reason with us. But don't ever let healthy reasoning become unhealthy or ungodly. Let peace be the umpire in your life (see Colossians 3:15). In other words, let peace be the deciding factor as to whether or not God is pleased with your questions.

When There Seems to Be No Way

Fear will take over if we allow ourselves to be convinced that there is no solution to our problem. How often do we say or hear others say, "There is just no way this is going to work out"? Just because we don't know the way doesn't mean that there is no way. Jesus said of Himself, "I am the Way" (John 14:6). Isaiah said God "will lead the blind by ways they have not known" (Isaiah 42:16 [NIV]). God is capable of leading us in the dark, because the dark is the same as light to Him. We may be in the dark about what is going on, but God is light so He never dwells in darkness. The psalmist David, in writing one of the greatest chapters in the Bible about trusting God completely, said:

> *Just because we don't know the way doesn't mean that there is no way.*

> If I take the wings of the morning or dwell in the uttermost parts of the sea,
>
> Even there shall Your hand lead me, and Your right hand shall hold me.
>
> If I say, Surely the darkness shall cover me and the night shall be [the only] light about me,
>
> Even the darkness hides nothing from You, but the night shines as the day; the darkness and the light are both alike to You.
>
> Psalm 139:9–12 (AMPC)

When we have had a long season of trials, or we are facing something extremely difficult, it is not uncommon to become discouraged and start thinking that this is going to be our permanent condition in life. We think things like: *This is never going to stop. I've done everything I know to do and nothing is working. There just seems to be no way!* But God has a different story to tell. He says:

> Do not [earnestly] remember the former things; neither consider the things of old.
>
> Behold, I am doing a new thing! Now it springs forth; do you not perceive and know it and will you not give heed to it? I will even make a way in the wilderness and rivers in the desert.
>
> Isaiah 43:18–19 (AMPC)

These Scriptures have encouraged me many different times in my life, and I pray they will do the same for you. When you're hurting, remember that *God will make a way!*

Think of a time in your life when He has made a way for you when there seemed to be no way, and remember that He will do it again! His ways are not our ways, but as Isaiah said, He can make a way even in a wilderness, and He can bring a river in the desert times of our lives.

Even when we decide to believe that He will make a way, it may bring us to another question: "When will He do it?" Only God knows for sure, and most of the time when we ask Him, He doesn't seem interested in giving us an answer. That must be because He wants us to trust Him.

CHAPTER 15

In God's Waiting Room (Part 1)

The two most powerful warriors are patience and time.

Leo Tolstoy

If you are anything like me, learning to be patient is one of the bigger challenges in life.

Have you ever been in a hospital waiting room where family and friends are waiting for the doctor to bring them word about someone they love who has had surgery? Most of the people waiting seem a bit anxious and the looks on their faces tend to be intense and show signs of concern. They are waiting to be told an outcome, but currently they know nothing. They are waiting and waiting and waiting. Will the news be good or will it be bad? If the wait is several hours longer than expected, those waiting may become even more anxious. Their thoughts may become darker and more negative, and in the natural world that would be understandable.

The big question is, how are we when we are in God's waiting room? Are we anxious, intense, and worried, or are we patiently waiting and expecting good news? If our wait is a lot longer than we thought it would be, do we remain positive and hopeful? We often say that we trust God, but are we showing the fruit of trusting Him?

God Has Forever to Work Things Out

God rarely seems to be in a hurry about anything, and we are usually in a hurry about everything! We are not satisfied to know that God will make a way; we want to know *when* He will make a way. The Scriptures promise us that at the appointed time, God will do what needs to be done, but when is the appointed time? It is the time that God determines is the right time, and He rarely ever lets us know how long that will be. We can, however, be assured that it won't be too long. Our Lord knows what we are capable of, and He will never push us past that point!

What we think is a long time is only a short time in God's way of looking at things:

> Nevertheless, do not let this one fact escape your notice, beloved, that with the Lord one day is like a thousand years, and a thousand years is like one day.
>
> 2 Peter 3:8

God sees things in light of eternity; therefore, He isn't in a hurry. He sees the end from the beginning. God has already been where we are going, and He already knows exactly what will happen! He always has a good reason for what He does, and learning to believe that helps us to trust Him whether our wait is short or long.

We often want things before we are mature enough to handle them properly, but God knows the best time, and I can assure you that He won't give us anything until the time is right. God may say, "Wait," or He may even say, "No," but whatever He decides will be the perfect thing done at the perfect time. Everything God does concerning our lives and our relationship with Him is for our good!

As children of God, we have the fruit of patience in us, according to Galatians 5:22, but it usually takes several years of walking with God before we see much of it manifested. It is deposited in us as a seed, but it takes time and experience in order to grow and become strong.

The root of the Greek word translated "patience" means to "abide under"—in other words, to stick with something even though it might be unpleasant or even painful. It means to see things all the way through to the finish. Most of us want to run from things that cause us any kind of suffering. The thought of enduring difficulty without at least knowing how long we are expected to do so is very unpleasant. God doesn't always give us the answers we desire when we want them, simply because He is committed to our spiritual growth, and He views that as much more important than our getting instant relief from something we are going through.

Before I knew much at all about trusting God, it really frustrated me when I needed God to do something that I knew would be quite easy for Him and yet He seemed to be doing nothing at all. I now realize that even though nothing was changing in my circumstances, God was working in me. He was stretching my faith, and by doing so, He was expanding it and making it stronger. Because I did not know how to trust God, I was miserable the entire time I had to wait, and I am sure my wait was much longer than it would have been had I known how to trust Him.

Life does get easier as we gain more experience with God. We learn that although He is usually not early, He truly is never late—at least not according to His timetable. Patience is not merely the ability to wait, it is also how we behave while we wait. We will all wait on many things in life, but to "wait patiently" is the goal God has in mind for us. Waiting patiently is simply not possible unless we trust that God's character is without flaw, and that He is good and displays His goodness to us as long as we live. Just because a thing does not "feel" good to me does not mean it is not good. I may eventually see that what I thought was bad was, in the long run, very good for me.

It Is Never Too Late

Martha and Mary sent a message to Jesus letting Him know that their brother Lazarus was ill. Scripture says that Jesus loved Martha, Mary, and Lazarus, and that they were His dear friends. That being said, even when He heard that Lazarus was sick, He stayed two more days where He was before He went to see him (see John 11:3–6). By the time Jesus arrived, Lazarus had died and had been in the tomb four days already. The natural question would be, "If Jesus loved them so much, why did He wait before going to help them?"

He waited because He wanted the situation to seem like one that was impossible to fix by the time He arrived. When Jesus got there, Martha said, "Lord, if You had been here, my brother would not have died" (John 11:21). We often think or say the same thing regarding our own circumstances: "Jesus, if You had wanted to, You could have prevented this from happening." We, of course, are disappointed and lack understanding on why God would allow something painful that He could have prevented, just as Martha did.

If you are familiar with the story of Lazarus, you know that

Jesus did not see the fact that Lazarus had been dead for several days as an insurmountable obstacle. In fact, He wanted the situation to appear impossible, so that the relatives and friends of Lazarus, as well as us, might learn that with God, all things are possible and it is never too late for Him to do what needs to be done. Jesus raised Lazarus from the dead, and I am sure after witnessing the miracle, everyone was glad it happened the way it did. Although I have never personally seen anyone raised from the dead, I have seen God give life to many dead circumstances and situations. I think this story should be viewed as an example of the truth that it is never too late for God to work wonders in our lives.

Instead of wanting God to do things our way, we can remember that His way is always better than ours in the long run. There are many mysteries hidden in the wisdom of God. We don't always understand *why* things happen as they do, but we do have the privilege of trusting God, and that makes our pain bearable.

Patience Is Power

Patience gives us the power to enjoy life while we wait for the things we desire. Much of life is wasted being miserable about things that we cannot change. If we can change something unpleasant, then we should do that, but if we cannot, then we should trust God and be determined not to be miserable while we wait to see what He will do. Each day we waste is one we will never get back, and a wise and prudent person does not waste any of the time God has allotted him to be on this earth.

> *Much of life is wasted being miserable about things that we cannot change.*

Frustration, discouragement, and misery have never made a

bad situation good, but they have caused illness, shortened lives, and ruined relationships. The apostle James said that a patient man is "perfectly and fully developed...lacking in nothing" (James 1:4 [AMPC]). Wow! That sure sounds good to me, and I am sure it does to you also. When I read that Scripture I am often tempted to think, *I wish I was patient, but I just am not there yet*, but we can be free from impatience. There is a way, and the way is through right thinking.

If I think that I must have what I want before I can be happy, then my own thinking is setting me up for misery. But if I change my thinking to, *I trust God and I know His timing is perfect; therefore, I will enter His rest and enjoy my life while I am waiting*, then I lack nothing as far as the moment I am in is concerned. Whatever God is going to do about our problems is not going to be hurried by our impatience. One thing is for certain—no matter how long we wait on God to act on our behalf, patience has the power to keep us joyful while we wait!

Something is always happening even when we think that nothing is happening. Consider how a tree grows. We cannot see it grow, but it is growing. It gets taller, and the branches get wider. They say that slow-growing trees bear the best fruit, and I think the same principle applies to people. We may not always see our branches getting wider, but our roots are getting deeper. Someday we will bear good fruit and realize that we were growing all the while we waited.

Forget It!

If we watch anything too closely, we cannot see its growth, but if we are away from it for a while and then return, we are amazed by it. My family had a piece of property that we needed to sell, and although it had been on the market for over three years, absolutely nothing was happening. Not only were we not selling it, but no one had even looked at it. We did not have a single offer in over three years, not even a bad one! I was frustrated because I *really* wanted to sell it. I prayed about it a lot, and declared by faith that it was sold. And each day that it didn't sell, I felt frustrated when I thought about it. One morning, as I started to pray about it again, the Lord spoke to my heart and said, *Just forget about that piece of property and let Me take care of it.* I realized right away that I had been spending an excessive amount of time focusing on that one thing, and God wanted me to get it off of my mind and simply trust that He was working.

> We often think we are waiting on God, but in reality, He may be waiting on us!

Each time the sale of the property came to my mind I thought, *God is taking care of it!* I finally entered God's rest concerning it, and within two weeks the property was sold! I'd like to say that I was patient while I was waiting those three years, but the fact is I wasn't, and my impatience may well have been the reason it took so long. We often think we are waiting on God, but in reality, He may be waiting on us!

The fear of not getting what we want is one of the main reasons for our impatience, but once again let me say that we can change our thinking and it will help us immensely. Instead of thinking, *Nothing is happening,* we can think, *I don't see anything happening, but I believe God is working!*

God knows everything that has happened in the past, is happening right now, and will happen in the future, and He is in control of all of it—He isn't anxious or impatient. Our impatience comes from the fact that we don't know how or when our answer will come. The less information we have, the easier it is to become impatient in God's waiting room, but the Word of God and experience tell us that His timing is perfect and the waiting that we dislike so much is actually working good things in us.

We read stories in the Bible of those we refer to as great men and women of God, and most of us have secretly wished that their testimonies were ours. At least we would like to be admired as they are, although we probably don't wish we had their experiences. They are indeed great, but let me remind you that they all waited in God's waiting room. Moses waited forty years in the wilderness. David waited twenty years to become king, and for fifteen of them he had to hide in caves to prevent Saul from killing him. Joseph waited thirteen years for his deliverance, and ten of them he spent in prison. Abraham waited twenty years before having the child God promised Him. If you and I stay in God's waiting room, we may one day have a great testimony that someone will read about and admire!

CHAPTER 16

In God's Waiting Room (Part 2)

Wait and hope for and expect the Lord; be brave and of good courage and let your heart be stout and enduring. Yes, wait for and hope for and expect the Lord.

Psalm 27:14 (AMPC)

It is very common for people to misunderstand what it truly means to wait on God. We may see waiting as a passive, non-active time when our life is put on hold. Most of us have a difficult time doing absolutely nothing, and if we view waiting on God in the wrong way, we may find that our misunderstanding leaves us disabled when it comes to actually doing it.

A deeper study of the original language that we get our word "wait" from reveals that waiting on God is actually intended to be very active spiritually. Although God may ask us to be still as far as trying to change our circumstances is concerned, He is not asking us to do nothing. He wants us to have an attitude of expectancy regarding what He is doing, and He wants us to be hopeful and expect Him to do a marvelous work in our lives. He wants us to thank Him for what He is doing even before we see it with our natural eyes.

Our thoughts and attitudes can keep us very joyful while we

are in God's waiting room, if we manage them properly. Consider these two types of thinking and see which one you believe would produce joy:

There is this type of thinking:

- *I've been waiting so long that I just don't think I can wait much longer.*
- *Nothing is happening!*
- *I feel like God has forgotten all about me.*
- *I'm afraid there is no answer for my problem.*
- *I might as well just give up.*

And there is this type of thinking:

- *I'm so excited to see what God is going to do.*
- *I believe God is working even though I don't see a change yet.*
- *God loves me and I know He will take care of my problem.*
- *Psalm 139 says that God is thinking about me all the time, so I know He has not forgotten me.*
- *I will not live in fear and I will never give up!*

It is very obvious which type of thinking would produce the most joy. That being the case, why do we tend toward negative thoughts and attitudes? The mind of the flesh, spoken of by the apostle Paul in Romans 8:6 (AMPC), "is sense and reason without the Holy Spirit," and it is based on reasoning and logic that leads to sin; therefore, if we follow it, we have no option but to make decisions based on how things in our circumstances look. But if we think with the mind of the Spirit, which is spoken of in the same verse, we are promised life and peace in our soul. With the mind of the Spirit, we can think as God does, and our thoughts will be filled with hope no matter how things might look.

What Are You Looking At?

We can think with the mind of the flesh or the mind of the Spirit, and the choice is ours. Sadly, many people live their entire lives merely thinking whatever drops into their minds, never realizing that their enemy, Satan, is the source of all their negative, hopeless, fearful, and doubt-filled thinking. They never realize that they can do their own thinking if they choose to by casting down wrong thoughts that don't agree with God's Word and replacing them with ones that do.

In 2 Corinthians chapter 4, Paul describes a time when he and other believers in Christ experienced very difficult circumstances. He said they were "hedged in (pressed) on every side [troubled and oppressed in every way], but not cramped or crushed . . . perplexed and unable to find a way out, but not driven to despair . . . pursued (persecuted and hard driven), but not deserted [to stand alone] . . . struck down to the ground but never struck out and destroyed" (4:8–9 [AMPC]). He also tells us why:

> Since we consider and look not to the things that are seen but to the things that are unseen; for the things that are visible are temporal (brief and fleeting), but the things that are invisible are deathless and everlasting.
>
> 2 Corinthians 4:18 (AMPC)

Paul and the people he ministered to knew they had bad circumstances, and I am sure they saw them, but they were also looking at something else. They saw Jesus and His promises of deliverance and victory. They looked not only with the natural eye, but with the spiritual eye. They looked with their hearts at the things they could not see with their natural eyes, yet they believed they were very real.

We believe in God, even though we cannot see Him with our natural eyes. We believe in angels, we believe in gravity, and on cloudy days when we cannot see it, we believe the sun is there. There are actually many things that we strongly believe in although we don't see them, so why can't we believe that God is working while we are waiting even though we don't see any evidence yet? We simply have not trained ourselves to do so, but that can change.

Our real life is within us. What goes on inside of us (our thoughts and attitudes) is more important than our circumstances. No matter how difficult our circumstances are around us, if we maintain a good attitude and dwell on positive thoughts based on God's Word, we can experience peace and joy. I believe a person incarcerated in prison who has learned to think positively and has a good attitude can be freer than a person who is living out in society but is filled with hatred, bitterness, and a negative attitude. Anyone can improve the quality of his life immediately simply by thinking on things that are good and maintaining an attitude of hope.

We can have good circumstances, lots of money, a good job, and a good family, yet still have a miserable life if we are ungrateful, selfish, and perhaps angry toward someone who offended us. But we can also have difficult circumstances, live alone, and have barely enough money to get by, yet still have peace and joy if we are thankful and spend our time trying to be a blessing to others.

> *Your attitude and thoughts belong to you, and nobody can make you have bad ones if you don't want to!*

Your attitude and thoughts belong to you, and nobody can make you have bad ones if you don't want to!

There is no evidence in Scripture that Joseph had anything other than hope and a good attitude during his thirteen years of waiting on God to bring deliverance to him. He had a dream for his life and he did not give up on it even though nothing in his circumstances indicated that it would ever come true. (You can read the story of Joseph in Genesis 37–50.)

Abraham waited twenty years to see the fulfillment of the promise that God gave him that he would have a child. Twenty years is a long time to be in God's waiting room.

I am certain that he had many opportunities to give up, but we find in Scripture that even though he had no reason to hope, he hoped in faith that his dreams would come true and that he would see the fulfillment of God's promises. Even when he considered (looked at and thought about) the impotence of his own body and the barrenness of Sarah's womb, no unbelief or distrust made him waver concerning the promise of God. He grew strong as he gave praise and glory to God. Praise is a narrative or tale of the goodness of God, so Abraham must have been thinking of the things that God had done for him throughout his life. Glory is the manifestation of all the excellence of God, so once again Abraham must have been considering and pondering all the great things God had done in the past. His choice to remember and think on good things kept him strong while he was in God's waiting room (see Romans 4:18–21).

Are you in God's waiting room right now in your life? Have you perhaps been there a long, long time? Has it been much longer than you expected it would be? How well are you waiting? What are your thoughts, and what is your attitude? I urge you to choose thoughts and attitudes that will enable you to wait patiently on God who does all things well.

Waiting with Hope

Thankfully, hope is not something we must wait to *feel* in order to have it. It is something we can decide to have no matter how difficult our circumstances may seem. God promises that if we will become prisoners of hope, He will restore double our former blessings to us (see Zechariah 9:12). In other words, if you are willing to be locked up with hope to the point where you are so hopeful that no matter what happens you cannot stop hoping, then God will restore anything that you have lost in your life and give you a double blessing.

Hope is not merely wishing things will turn out well; it is a force of power that produces breakthroughs when we diligently hold on to it. While we are waiting, one of the most helpful things we can do to keep us strong in faith and filled with hope is diligently study and meditate on God's Word (His promises). The Word of God has power inherent in it that will encourage and empower those who put their hope in Him.

The psalmist David, a young man who also waited twenty years to see the promise that God gave him come to pass, said this:

> I wait for the Lord, I expectantly wait, and in His word do I hope.
>
>   Psalm 130:5 (AMPC)

Hope needs to have a basis. There needs to be a reason to hope, and David said that his reason was the Word of God. David simply put His trust in God's faithfulness to fulfill His Word.

Why is the study and meditation of God's Word so helpful? It is seed, and seed always produces after its own kind. When the Word is sown in a heart that is fertile ground (meek and tender), it cannot do anything other than produce a harvest. We see this principle throughout the Word of God, but Mark chapter 4 gives us insight into this truth. Speaking of seeds, it says the following:

> And those sown on the good (well-adapted) soil are the ones who hear the Word and receive and accept and welcome it and bear fruit—some thirty times as much as was sown, some sixty times as much, and some [even] a hundred times as much.
>
> Mark 4:20 (AMPC)

I strongly urge you to read, study, listen to, and meditate on God's Word as often as possible, and do so with a believing heart, one that is meek (gentle and kind). James tells us that when the Word is "implanted and rooted" in our hearts, it has the power to save our souls (see James 1:21 [AMPC]). God's Word changes us and enables us to be what God wants us to be and to do what He wants us to do. When we are in His waiting room, He does not want us to give up, and His Word will give us the power to stand strong until His appointed time comes for our breakthrough.

Put your hope in God and in His Word! Expect to hear good news at any moment! When we live with hope, we can see deliverance from our problems, and we can enjoy the journey.

Be Obedient While You Wait

> Wait for and expect the Lord and keep and heed His way, and He will exalt you to inherit the land...
>
> Psalm 37:34 (AMPC)

Waiting with hope is one aspect of successfully seeing victory in our lives, but waiting and keeping His ways is another aspect that must be considered. Hopefully, we all know the importance of obedience, but we should also realize that no matter how difficult it might be in good times, it is even more difficult when we find ourselves in God's waiting room, enduring difficult circumstances, and we have not seen any change in a long time. During those times, we don't always feel like doing the right things—like being kind and loving to others, or serving and giving.

Displaying the fruit of the Spirit is much more difficult when we have stress and pressure in our lives. It can even be difficult to want to pray or study God's Word; however, these are the times when it is the most important. Doing the right thing while the right thing is not happening to us is possibly one of the most powerful things that we can do. Paul tells us not to be weary in doing what is right, for in due time we shall reap if we don't faint (see Galatians 6:9). I want to take time to encourage you to keep on doing what is right while you are in God's waiting room! Do it because you love Him and because you appreciate all that He has done and is doing for you even right now.

> *Doing the right thing while the right thing is not happening to us is possibly one of the most powerful things that we can do.*

God wants us to walk by faith, and walking by faith means that we walk not by sight or how we feel, but by what we know to be right. And doing what is right simply because it is right is a very powerful thing. It clearly declares that we trust God and are committed to honoring Him with our actions no matter what our circumstances may be.

When we are steadfast and immovable, always abounding in the work of the Lord, we are promised that our work will not be in vain (see 1 Corinthians 15:58). God always sees faithfulness, even if no one else does. And those who remain steadfast during trials will receive the victor's crown of life (see James 1:12).

Let us trust God and look forward to our reward, even while we are in God's waiting room. Let us expect good things to happen to us, and let us rejoice in our hope that all things are possible with God!

CHAPTER 17

When God Is Silent

Keep not silence, O God; hold not Your peace or be still, O God.

Psalm 83:1 (AMPC)

I've thought many times, *I wish God would come and sit here with me and just tell me what He wants me to do!* I am sure you have thought something similar at some time in your life. It seems to me that it would make things a lot easier, but it appears that God has different ideas, because that is not what He chooses to do. If He doesn't want to do things our way, then we will have to learn how to do them His way. He wants us to trust Him even when He is silent!

Do you ever feel that God has packed up, moved far away, and left no forwarding address? When we don't see God doing anything in our life, and we don't hear Him saying anything, we may feel as if we are groping around in the dark, trying to find our way through a maze. Although these times challenge our faith, they can teach us an important lesson: to trust God even when He is silent. Just because He is silent does not mean that He isn't doing anything.

> *Do you ever feel that God has packed up, moved far away, and left no forwarding address?*

God was silent for four hundred years between the closing of the Old Testament and the opening of the New Testament, but there were things going on during that time that actually prepared the people for the coming of the Messiah. The Bible says that in the fullness of time Jesus was born! (See Galatians 4:4.) God always has a proper time for things. When He is ready, He will speak, and until He does, it is our job to keep listening and waiting with expectancy.

Let's consider what God's Word tells us about Elijah in 1 Kings 17:1. Elijah prophesied to the people that there would be no rain for several years, and sure enough, it did not rain for three years and six months. The people suffered from a severe drought, and it is quite likely that Elijah was not very popular during that time. I would imagine that he wanted to hear something new from God about the drought, but according to 1 Kings 18:1 (NIV), "after a long time, in the third year, the word of the Lord came to Elijah," giving him another instruction. This time he was to announce that rain was coming, and it did.

There are other examples of God being silent with those who trusted Him. He was silent with Job and with Abraham. The reading of Job chapter 23 gives clear insight into the desperation that Job felt at not being able to find God or hear from Him. Let's look at a few of the verses:

Oh, that I knew where I might find Him, that I might come even to His seat!

Job 23:3 (AMPC)

Behold, I go forward [and to the east], but He is not there; I go backward [and to the west], but I cannot perceive Him;

> On the left hand [and to the north] where He works [I
> seek Him], but I cannot behold Him; He turns Himself to
> the right hand [and to the south], but I cannot see Him.
> Job 23:8–9 (AMPC)

Now listen to Job's faith speak in the midst of this terrible
silence from God:

> But He knows the way that I take [He has concern for it,
> appreciates, and pays attention to it]. When He has tried
> me, I shall come forth as refined gold [pure and luminous].
> Job 23:10 (AMPC)

Even though Job could not see God or hear Him, he stated
that he believed God was watching over him and was concerned
about him. He spoke of "when" God would deliver him, not "if"
God would deliver him!

Abraham dealt with the silence of God regarding the surrender
of his only son, Isaac. God had instructed Abraham to sacrifice
his son as a way of testing his faithfulness and obedience, and He
waited until the last possible second to speak to Abraham, telling
him not to harm Isaac. But up until that moment, Abraham only
had raw faith to go by. He was so convinced of the faithfulness of
God, he felt that even if he did slay Isaac, God would raise him
from the dead (see Genesis 22:1–12).

I have not been through anything as extreme as what Job
or Abraham describes, but I have had long periods of silence
between times of hearing from God. These are difficult times
when we are tempted to think that God isn't with us or that He
doesn't care about us. We may also think that we have lost our
ability to hear from God.

I pressured myself for many years, taking the responsibility of "trying" to hear from God, but finally I realized that if God wanted to say something to me, He had many ways of making sure I knew what it was. Instead of *trying* to hear from God and feeling frustrated when you don't, trust that when God wants to speak to you, He will make Himself clearly known.

Instead of being afraid that you won't hear from God, believe you will hear from Him. If God knows that you truly want to hear His voice and that you are prepared to follow it, He will not fail to speak when the time is right. In the fullness of time, or at the appointed time, God spoke to Elijah again, and He will also speak to you again!

Six Things to Do When God Is Silent

1. *When God is silent, just keep doing what He told you to do the last time you believe you heard from Him.*

Paul taught the believers to stand fast in the liberties they had been given, and not to be ensnared again in a yoke of bondage (see Galatians 5:1). Hang on to what you have and don't allow a time of silence from God to discourage and weaken your faith.

There is a great deal that I don't know, but there is also a great deal that I do know, and I am actively doing all that I know to do at the current time in my life. I am frequently asked, "What is next for your ministry?" Since I cannot foretell the future, I don't usually know the answer to that. If we have something planned, I can report that, but, more often than not, I am simply doing what most of us do, and that is living each day as it comes and trusting God. What is next will be a surprise to me as well as to others.

Another question I am asked by many people is, "What is God

saying to you?" I am especially asked that question at the first of each year, as if because the page turned on the calendar I should now have a new revelation from God. Even though January 1 may be viewed as an opportunity to talk about doing new things, God doesn't always have some special new word just because it is the first day of the year. God is not a jukebox filled with options we can request from Him at certain times. He speaks when He chooses and as He chooses, and when He is silent, we keep doing what we know to do.

Dave and I were laughing with some friends recently because the woman said that when she and her husband first got married, he was excessively spiritual and he assigned her a certain amount of Bible reading each day. When he returned home from his job as an associate pastor at a local church, one of the first things he said to her was, "What did God show you today?" I can only imagine the type of pressure that put on her and how she must have felt like a failure if she had to say, "Nothing." It is funny now, but I doubt it was very funny at the time. Don't pressure yourself, or anyone else, to come up with a "word from God," unless you want to open a door for the devil to deceive you.

2. God's silence could be a compliment to you.

Perhaps He is not giving you any specific instructions because He trusts you to make the right decision. It is an error to believe that God will tell us each move we are to make. That kind of relationship is for parents and babies, not for mature sons and daughters. One of my sons said this morning, "I'll come by this afternoon, Mom." I have not sent him a list of instructions on exactly how I expect him to behave when he comes into the house. I trust him, and I trust that he knows my heart and will act accordingly. For example, he won't come in and leave the door open behind him. He won't park his car in a place that would prevent anyone else from getting their car out of the garage. He won't bring someone in the house with him that I don't know. I don't need to tell him those things, because he already knows my heart.

God gives us freedom to make decisions according to His Word and what we know of His will and character. I recently heard a well-known man of God say that God had never given him any specific instructions at any important intersection in his life. He found that at times when he had really important decisions to make, as he prayed for God's direction, he was led to step out and try various things until he had peace about the right thing. We must remember that even though God may seem to us to be silent, He is always communicating with us in a variety of ways—through His Word, peace, wisdom, our experience from the past, and other things.

> *If God isn't telling you exactly what you should do, then be confident that He trusts you to make the right decisions!*

If God isn't telling you exactly what you should do, then be confident that He trusts you to make the right decisions! It is impossible to drive a parked car, so there are times when we must put our lives in drive and start inching forward before we will find out if we are going in the right direction or not.

3. Don't compare yourself with anyone else!

We often hear people talk about how God has dealt with them and assume that God should deal with us the same way, but He doesn't. I have read books by people who make it sound as if God sits on the edge of their bed giving them daily instructions on what they are to do. "God said" and "God told me" are their favorite terms. I use those terms too, and perhaps more than I should, because there are times when people misunderstand what we mean. We can be continually led and guided by God, but that doesn't mean that we are getting a play-by-play media presentation of what we are to do all day long, each day.

I know people who seem to hear specifics more frequently from God than I do, but I have learned not to compare myself with anyone. If we do, then we can never be content in our own relationship with God. We are individuals, and God deals with us in different ways for different reasons, and we should trust that. When you are comfortable with a person, it is possible to sit in a room and not say a word. Some days it must be enough for us just to believe that God is with us!

4. Keep talking to God even if you don't think He is answering.

We need to express ourselves, and God wants to assure us that we can talk to Him about anything as often as we want or need to. The psalmist David certainly poured his heart out to God, and he did so with great honesty. Most of us have times when we just want someone to talk to. You may not care much what they have to say; you just want someone to listen and keep your secrets, and God is always good at that.

5. Keep listening, even if you have a long dry spell of not hearing anything.

Continuing to listen lets God know that your heart is open to Him and that you are waiting for Him. I ask God very often if

He has anything He wants to say to me, and I take a few minutes to just be quiet. It is my way of obeying what He said to us in Proverbs:

> In all your ways know, recognize, and acknowledge Him,
> and He will direct and make straight and plain your paths.
>
> Proverbs 3:6 (AMPC)

Even if I hear nothing when I ask that question, I still believe that my listening is valuable. I have found that God may be silent when I ask the question, but then He will direct my circumstances in such a way that it is very clear to me that He was involved in guiding the outcome of my situation.

6. Ask God to examine you.

David sometimes asked God to examine him to see if anything was in his heart that was not right (see Psalm 26:2, 139:23–24). This is a bold step, but one that clearly proves whether or not a person truly wants God's will, no matter what it might be.

Is it possible there is something blocking us from hearing God clearly? A sin, a wrong attitude, or a misunderstanding on how to hear from God could be hindering us. We don't need to be afraid to know the truth, because it will set us free. When God is silent, we may not be doing anything wrong, but there is no harm in finding out.

Although God was silent with Job for a long time, He did eventually answer him, but when He did, He had some things to say that Job probably wasn't expecting. Out of frustration, Job eventually told God that he didn't deserve the treatment he was getting, and more or less demanded some answers. Job indicated that he thought God was unjust in His treatment of him. He was not aware of the spiritual warfare that was going on behind the scenes, just as we are often not aware of what is going on behind the scenes. The Bible says that Job repented, so he obviously had sinned.

Although he was a righteous man in every way when his trials began, Job eventually assumed that God was not dealing with him properly (see Job 42:3–6). His righteousness turned into a type of self-righteousness that is dangerous for any of us to have. Job definitely went through a very hard time (certainly more than anyone we know of), but in the end, he said that he now knew God much better than he had previously (see Job 42:5). Also, God gave him back double everything he had lost and blessed him tremendously (see Job 42:10–17).

The journey was hard, but it turned out good in the end! This is the same thing we can expect. Remember: What Satan means for harm, God intends for good (see Genesis 50:20).

CHAPTER 18

Trusting God during Times of Change

Those who cannot change their minds cannot change anything.

George Bernard Shaw

Many people don't like change and aggressively resist it. But things in this world are always changing, whether we want them to or not, so refusing to accept it is useless. What we need to do is change our minds about how we think about change, because when that happens, life is easier to handle. Let's examine what some people think about change and why.

Some people emphatically say, "I hate change!" They may feel that way because they don't like being out of control or because they are insecure and afraid of new things, or even because they have a habit of thinking that they don't like change. Certain types of thinking can be habits that we have picked up from the people who influenced us in our childhood, or they can merely be strongholds that Satan has built in our minds to prevent us from having the best life Jesus wants us to have.

Change is a constant in all of our lives, and to resist it is like resisting the wind when it decides to blow. I have a granddaughter who is a planner, and anytime there is a change from what she had planned, it is difficult for her to adjust; it can even make her anxious. But nothing we do will keep change from taking

> *Change is a constant in all of our lives, and to resist it is like resisting the wind when it decides to blow.*

place, at least in some instances. There may be some changes we can prevent, but we may also be preventing something good that God has planned! We cannot get from where we are to where we want to be without change of some kind. It is impossible to keep doing what you have always done and get a different result. Some people want a different result than what they are experiencing, yet they aggressively resist change.

Change Your Mind about Change

If you don't like change, ask yourself why. You may find that even you don't understand the reasoning behind your attitude, and that simply changing your thinking will give you an entirely new perspective on change.

Here are some destructive ways we can think about change that do nothing more than make us miserable:

- *I hate change.*
- *I'm afraid of change.*
- *I don't like change.*
- *I like to be in control of what is happening in my life.*
- *I like the way things are right now, and I don't want them to change.*

Here are some constructive ways we can think about change that will help us navigate it with joy:

- *I like change.*
- *I believe the changes in my life will make things better.*
- *I'm excited about seeing the results of this change.*
- *I want to be all I can be and I know that change is part of the process.*
- *I want to be where God wants me to be and that may require change.*

We can all renew our minds by choosing to think thoughts that are in line with God's Word and will. He makes it clear in Scripture that only He never changes, and that everything else is subject to change (see Malachi 3:6; Hebrews 12:27).

When something changes, it doesn't necessarily mean that what was being done previously was wrong. It can also mean that something better is coming! We recently had an employee who resigned his position, giving us only two weeks' notice, and we had no one to replace him. His job was important and not one that would be easy to find a replacement for. I could feel the stress, but I continued to trust God to provide and to cause us to come up higher through this change—to make the new situation even better than the old one was.

As it turned out, we ended up not needing to replace the employee at all because two other men on his team stepped up and said, "We believe we can take on more responsibility and do the job with fewer people than before." It has worked out marvelously, and we could not be any happier with the change. So something we initially resisted and didn't like ended up being a blessing in a greater way than we had expected.

To everything there is a time, a season, and everything is beautiful in its time (see Daniel 2:21; Ecclesiastes 3:1, 11). In the Bible, we see that as long as the earth remains, there will be changing seasons (see Genesis 8:22). Winter gives way to spring, and spring to summer, and summer to fall, and fall to winter. The temperature, wind velocity, and humidity change daily. We expect change when it comes to the weather, but we also need to expect change in other areas of our lives, because it always happens. We change in many ways as we get older. The people around us change, their commitments may change, and as things change in their lives, it may necessitate changes in our relationships with them.

When our children grow up and leave home, our relationships with them will change, but they don't have to be less than what we want them to be; they just need to be different, and they can be better than ever.

My daughter dropped something off at the house the other day and I was in the mood for company and a girl chat, so when she started to leave only a few minutes after she arrived I said, "Why are you in such a hurry? Come and sit for a while." She responded with, "Mom, I have a family at home I want to get back to." I started drifting in the direction of getting my feelings hurt, but as I asked God to help me, I realized that she has many other responsibilities in her life besides visiting with me, and I should not make it difficult for her by being offended. I truly do want her to be free to live her life the way she needs to without any pressure from me. She spends lots of time with me and also does a lot for me, so for me to put pressure on her on the occasions when she is busy with her family would be selfish, and could potentially harm our good relationship. We have to let our children grow up and make their own decisions. And even though we may not like all of their choices, they are entitled to make them and we should respect that.

So often, people are absolutely miserable after their children leave home. It seems especially difficult for *Mom*. She has spent her life pouring her love and attention into her child, perhaps even too much of her life, and now the child is off doing new things and Mom is alone trying to find new direction. One response she can have is to keep pressuring her child to spend time with her and ruin her relationship with them, or put them in a position where they feel manipulated, so that anything they do for her is done not out of a desire to do it but as a duty with no joy in it. A much better response is to let her child go, developing a new relationship with them that is based largely on friendship rather than a mommy/child dynamic. After accepting that things are changing and beginning to think in a new way, she will find that God never closes one door without opening another—one that is beautiful in its time like the last one was.

A woman I know recently said, "The child I never thought would break my heart did, and the one I thought would, didn't!" People don't always do what we thought they would do, and when this happens, it's one of the best times in life to trust God. People may change in ways that are difficult for us, but even those times can work out for good if we keep a positive attitude and continue to trust God. Truly, trusting God is the key to everything. It allows us to enter God's rest and remain peaceful during the changing times in our lives.

God knows everything that has happened in the past, is happening right now, and will happen in the future, and He is in control of all of it, so He isn't anxious or impatient. Our impatience and worry come from the fact that we don't know many of the things we would like to know, especially during times of change, and it makes us feel uneasy. God, of course, could reveal everything that is going to happen in the future and let us know how the changes in our life will turn out, but He doesn't.

That is because He expects us to trust Him. It is our privilege to trust Him!

When we have unexpected change in our lives, or even planned changes, it often leaves us with many questions that only God has the answers to. We of course want to know the entire blueprint for our lives right now, but I have come to believe that if we knew everything that would take place in the future, life would either be boring as we live it out day by day, or more frightening than not knowing.

God is good, and it stands to reason that if knowing what is going to happen before it happens is the best thing for us, then God will arrange things to work that way. If He doesn't do that, we can safely assume that waiting and being surprised is the best thing for us. Trusting God means that we trust His ways. We should not merely trust Him to give us what *we* want, we must trust Him for *His* best in our lives, and that includes His timing and His way of dealing with us.

If you are a person who does not like change, I am recommending that you change your mind about change, because it often produces some of the most positive things in our life.

The Brook Dried Up

We may like our life just the way it is, but what if God decides it is time for change? And what if the thing He leads us to doesn't seem to be as good as what we had to leave? That seemingly happened to Elijah, but there is no mention of him not liking it or complaining about it.

Elijah lived in a time of severe drought, but God was miraculously taking care of him. He lived by a brook of running water and ravens brought him food each day. But eventually the brook dried up (see 1 Kings 17:7). God then told Elijah to go to another town where a widow would care for him. When he arrived, he found that the woman was down to her last meal and had planned for her and her son to eat it and die. It was a rather dismal situation, if you ask me, and certainly not one to be excited about, but as I said, there is no mention of any complaint from Elijah. He told the widow that if she would feed him first, her food supply would not run dry throughout the drought. She did as he said, and sure enough, they had plenty (see 1 Kings 17:8–16).

This change in Elijah's life wasn't necessarily one that benefited him, but it did benefit the widow. There have been times in my life, and there will be in yours, when God changes something in our lives in order to help someone else. It might not seem to help us, or we may even seem to have gone a step or two backward for a season, but He is using us as His agent of change in another person's life. When we have finished our assignment, we can trust that God will promote us to a place that's even better than the one we left behind.

I am quite sure that Jesus liked it much better when He was in Heaven with His Father before He came to earth to pay for our sins than He did when He was hanging on the cross, suffering and dying for us. Nevertheless, He gladly accepted the assignment because of the good that would be done for others. If we want to be used by God, some changes that we don't care for may be necessary from time to time.

If your brook dries up, don't be overly concerned. I can assure you that God has a new plan. For example, if a person loses his job because of company cutbacks that he wasn't expecting, he may feel frightened by the change that has been thrust upon him. This is understandable, but continuing to trust God during times of change is one of the keys to letting change push him forward.

Trusting God in any and every situation is the main ingredient to learning to live a life of peace, joy, and victory.

Wait Out the Storm

More than thirty years ago, I left a ministry position at a local church to follow what I believed to be the leading of God. I had good ministry opportunities at the church, but I felt I would have even more opportunities in a different situation. For quite a while it seemed as if the change I made wasn't producing as well as what I had left behind. Actually, it seemed as if I had gone backward instead of forward.

Eventually things changed, proving that I had indeed made the right decision, but it took more time than I had thought it would. If you are in a season of change and it seems that things are not working out, just be patient and continue being faithful to do what you feel God is leading you to do. It would be a shame if you gave up right before your breakthrough. Think of it this way: When it is stormy outside we often have to remain inside and just wait it out before continuing with our plans.

Some changes in our life may seem like storms. They are sudden and unexpected and may hinder us from doing what we had planned to do. Not all storms are in the weather forecast! Emotions flare during times of change, and we need to wait for them to subside before making any decisions. I don't think it is wise to make decisions during emotional highs or lows. We need time to adjust to changes, time to think, and time to hear from God. Before you make any major decisions during times of change, I strongly recommend that you simply wait. Give

Before you make any major decisions during times of change, I strongly recommend that you simply wait.

yourself time to get used to the new way of doing things, or the new responsibility, or the new people in your life. While you are waiting, set your mind in a positive direction. Believe that good things are going to happen, and keep a good attitude!

Things seem to find a place to settle into our lives if we just give them time. I remember a time when some of our key leaders at the ministry wanted to make a change that I wasn't particularly excited about, but I decided, out of respect for them, to go along with it. I really didn't like it for quite some time, and occasionally had to resist negative and critical feelings that I knew God didn't approve of. It took several months, but I finally settled in with the change. I could have followed my feelings and insisted that we abandon the change because I just didn't like it, and I have the authority to do that. But deep down inside, I knew that wasn't the way to go, so I waited! The storm inside of me ended, and things were peaceful once again. It turned out that the changes were very good, and in the end I was glad I had followed the advice of my coworkers.

Maybe you don't like a change at work that you cannot do anything about or a change in some other circumstance or person in your life. But if you decide to make the best of it, you too may eventually find that the new situation is better after all.

I recently got my hair cut shorter than it has ever been, and at first I didn't like it, but now I love it. I think it makes me look younger, and it is much easier to take care of! Dave had a mustache for forty years, and one day he came out of the bathroom with it shaved off. It looked to me like his lip was missing, and for a long time I really didn't like it. But now I love it and think he looks younger that way, and I wouldn't want him to grow it back. The point I am trying to make is that we need to give things time, and when we do, quite often we will adapt and actually like the changes of life.

CHAPTER 19

I Really Want to Change

Everyone thinks of changing the world, but no one thinks of changing himself.

Leo Tolstoy

There are some things in life that we want to change, and we would be very happy if God were to decide to change those things. But what if *we* are the ones who need to change?

I wasted a lot of years thinking that if my circumstances or the people around me would change, then I could be happier. I tried to change them, I prayed for God to change them, but then I discovered that God wanted to change me. Up to that point, I had not considered that *I* needed to change, and that this was the solution to some of the unhappiness and discontentment in my life. When I finally did take a good honest look at myself, I realized that nothing and nobody could ever make me happy until I became happy with myself. I really didn't like who I was, but I had spent so much time trying to put the blame for my unhappiness on other people and things that I had entirely missed the truth.

Satan likes for us to focus on what is wrong with others, because that way we never see what is wrong with us. Our judgment of them blinds us to our own faults. It has been very helpful for me to realize that when my time here on earth is up, I will stand before God and only be required to give an account of myself (see Romans 14:12). He won't ask me about anyone else, just me. Therefore, I should focus on letting God do what He wants to do in me, instead of trying to get Him to change someone or something else.

When God is dealing with us about behaviors or attitudes that He doesn't approve of, it can be very confusing. God's Word refers to this process as "conviction," and it is the work of the Holy Spirit. We may simply feel that "something is wrong," but we don't know what it is. Instead of trying to figure out what it is, I highly recommend trusting God! The more we live in the realm of the mind, the less we are able to discern and truly comprehend what God wants to show us.

Let's say I am arguing with Dave about something, and although I feel uncomfortable in my spirit, it doesn't occur to me that the Holy Spirit is trying to convict me of wrong behavior, simply because I am thoroughly convinced that I am right about my opinion and that Dave is wrong.

Until we learn to promptly recognize those feelings for what they are, we may resist the work of the Holy Spirit and not be aware of what we are doing. But as we trust God to show us truth, we will learn, and the truth will make us free. I believe it is wise to regularly pray that we will not be deceived in any area of our lives, and that God will change and transform us into the image of Jesus Christ (see Romans 8:29–30).

Are You Willing to Change?

I believe in destiny, but I don't think it is an automatic outcome, totally controlled by God, that we have nothing to do with. God has an assignment for each one of us, but we more than likely will need to be changed before He can use us the way He wants to. I was very excited about God's call on my life to teach His Word, but I initially had no idea how much He would have to do *in* me before He could work *through* me.

God has a good plan for each of us, but there are times when we get off course and go in a wrong direction. Thankfully, with God's help, we can always make a course correction. We can even see our mistakes turned into blessings by following God's guidance. Two men in the Bible who were headed in the wrong direction are Jacob and Paul. But as God worked in their lives, they both changed, and even though they made many serious mistakes, they ended up with amazing lives.

Jacob was a trickster, swindler, and schemer who became a great man of God (see Genesis 32:22–28), and Paul was a persecutor of Christians who became a great apostle (see Acts 7:58; 8:1–3; 9:1, 4, 17, 22). It is never too late to change and see your destiny fulfilled.

> It is never too late to change and see your destiny fulfilled.

Many times, in order to experience the changes we would like to have in our circumstances, *we* must be willing to change first. Both Jacob and Paul not only experienced changes in their circumstances, but they embraced the changes that needed to be made in themselves. I want to recommend that if you are not happy with the way your life is going, before you ask God to change your life, ask Him to change anything in you that needs to change. Let us become who God wants us to be and before long, we will be doing what He wants us to do, and we'll have what He wants us to have. Being transformed into the image of Christ can be a long and painful journey, but it can definitely go more smoothly and quickly if we cooperate with the Holy Spirit as He works in us.

Sometimes in your journey, it may feel as if you are the only one who needs to change. It was especially difficult for me when I felt I was the only one whom God was dealing with. One time when I was complaining to Him about it, He whispered in my heart, "Joyce, you have asked Me for a lot; do you want it or not?" God, of course, does deal with all of us, or at least He attempts to, but not all of us listen and embrace the changes He wants to make in us. I really want to encourage you to never be overly concerned about what God is or isn't doing in someone else's life, but accept what He is doing in yours.

If God is working in you at this time in your life, it may seem as if you are not the person you once were, but you are not yet who you are going to be, and you feel as if you are stuck! You can't go back, and you can't go forward without God helping you, and He seems to be taking a nap. Now is not the time to give up—continue trusting God! Trusting God is not a one-time, five-second thing, but a day-in and day-out journey. God changes us little by little. And oftentimes we cannot even discern that change is taking place until we look back over a long period of time and observe that we truly are different than we used to be. I frequently say, "I'm not where I need to be, but thank God I am not where I used to be!"

I had some very serious personality dysfunction after being abused by my father, and even after I admitted it and wanted to change, it still took a long time. Don't be discouraged if your progress seems slow; just believe that God knows what He is doing, and enjoy yourself while you are changing. Remember—being miserable does not make change go faster!

During our journey of spiritual maturity, we will need to trust God's timing and His ways even though they probably won't be what we would have chosen. However, many years from now, when you look back on your life, you will realize they were perfect!

Being transformed into the image of Christ is the greatest change of all, and it traverses many seasons in our life, but each one is truly beautiful in its time. God has a program

> *Being transformed into the image of Christ is the greatest change of all.*

designed especially for each of us. So enjoy each season, enjoy God, and enjoy yourself as you make the journey!

Learning to Do Things Differently

As I ponder the wonderful changes God has made in me over the years, I realize that each one required that I learn how to do things differently, or how to respond to circumstances differently than I once did.

For example, I used to be very selfish, but once God revealed to me the depth of my selfishness and how many problems it was causing in my life, I truly wanted to change. But "self-will" dies slowly, and it is often quite painful. It took me a long time just to see the depth of my selfishness, and even longer to learn to stay happy and keep a good attitude when things didn't go my way. The more I learned to trust God, the easier it became, but it sure didn't happen overnight!

I learned that in order to enjoy peace, I had to adapt myself to people and things, instead of always expecting them to adapt to me (see Romans 12:16). It took a few years for me to fully realize that having peace was actually better than getting my own way all the time. Peace is one of the most precious things we can have, and we would be wise to prize it highly. Do you want peace enough to make whatever changes you have to make in order to have it?

I also learned that being right is highly overrated, and if I have to lose my peace in order to try and prove I am right when I disagree with someone, it simply isn't worth it. We can trust God to prove us right if that is what is needed, and if not, then we can choose to be content either way.

The learning process is never-ending. We continue learning all throughout life in many areas, and learning to follow God's ways is no different. I am still learning daily about my relationship with Him, and I am sure you are as well.

The Process of Change

Once we decide we want to change and we're willing to let the Holy Spirit work in our lives, there is an important lesson that we all must learn: We cannot change ourselves by ourselves, and true change requires trusting God to do the work in us that needs to be done. Most of us struggle and end up frustrated and disappointed because we try to change and fail. We make a little progress, and then it seems we fall right back into old habits. So we decide to try harder, or we develop new plans and formulas on how we can change, but we still don't succeed.

If we want to change and we try to change, then why can't we change? Why can't we simply stop doing something that we don't want to do? For example, if I am convinced that I speak without thinking and it is causing problems in my relationships, so I *want* to change that trait in me, why can't I do it? The answer is simple: We can't succeed without God. He wants us to ask for and receive His help in all that we do. Only God can truly change us, because it is an inside job.

If we try really hard to keep quiet and not cause arguments by saying wrong things, we may succeed for a while, but in an unguarded moment the problem will show up again. But if we learn to trust God to help us in all of our communication, we will find that little by little, He changes us. One day we realize that old problem is no longer a problem, and we cannot do anything except thank God because we know that He did it. Only those who abide in Christ will experience true change! God's plan is this: "If you remain in me and I in you, you will bear much fruit; apart from me you can do nothing" (John 15:5 [NIV]).

It's human nature to want to do things ourselves so we can be proud of ourselves, but God wants us to trust Him in all things and then give Him thanks for all that He has done.

Are you struggling with yourself? Are you trying to change things about yourself that you don't like or things that you know are not in agreement with God's will? Perhaps you worry and you are *trying* not to worry, or maybe you're angry with someone and you're *trying* to forgive them. It could be a thousand different things, but the one thing we must learn is that we cannot change merely by trying; we need God's help.

Thankfully, we can pray and put our trust and confidence in Him to do what needs to be done in us. Any effort we make must be made while leaning on God, not apart from Him. This sounds simple, but it is one of the most difficult things for us to learn, simply because human flesh is very independent. We will have to trade our independence for dependence on Jesus if we ever want to have true success. Learn to lean! Learn to trust!

> We will have to trade our independence for dependence on Jesus if we ever want to have true success.

The apostle Paul shares with us in Romans 7:15–25 that he tried and failed until he learned that only God could deliver him and that He would do it through Christ. After what appears to be quite a struggle that Paul was having with himself as he tried to do right and continued failing, he said:

> O unhappy and pitiable and wretched man that I am! Who will release and deliver me from [the shackles of] this body of death?
>   O thank God! [He will!] through Jesus Christ (the Anointed One) our Lord! . . .
>
> Romans 7:24–25 (AMPC)

It seems clear to me from the language and punctuation we find in these verses that Paul was quite emphatic and sure that he had finally found the right answer. Only God could do what needed to be done in him, and only God can do what needs to be done in us!

Ask and Receive

If you want to change, then God sees that and He is pleased! Now the next step is trusting Him to do what needs to be done and to give you the strength you need to change. All too often, when we want to change, we try to do it while totally leaving God out of the entire process. It won't work! It didn't work for the apostle Paul and it won't work for us. The bottom line here is we must trust God to work His will in us instead of trying to do it ourselves.

James 4:6 says that God "gives us more and more grace [through the power of the Holy Spirit to defy sin and live an obedient life that reflects both our faith and our gratitude for our salvation]." Grace is God's favor and enabling power, and without a constant flow of it in our lives, we end up frustrated and worn out.

I remember how elated I was when I discovered this truth. I

had tried so hard to be what I thought God wanted me to be, but I continually failed and was confused and disappointed. I tried and failed thousands of times. I said I was giving up, but then I got my determination back again and tried and failed some more. But when I finally learned that God's grace was the missing ingredient in my plans and I began trusting Him to change me, I started having victories.

Like the hymn says, "Amazing Grace! How sweet the sound!" But we must ask God for His grace in our lives. James 4:2 says, "...You do not have because you do not ask [it of God]." That is so simple! Ask! Ask and receive "that your joy may be full and complete" (John 16:24). When I was struggling to change, I was trying, but I wasn't asking...I wasn't trusting. Trusting God is usually the missing ingredient in all of our failures. If we'll trade all of our fleshly trying for more trusting in God, we'll be amazed at the results!

What Is Our Part?

We are taught in God's Word that as we look steadfastly into the Word of God, we are changed into Christ's image from glory to glory (see 2 Corinthians 3:18). Our part is to study God's Word and trust that it has the power to change us. Take the Word into your heart like medicine and trust it to do its work. James said that the Word of God has the power to save our souls (see James 1:21).

Trusting God's Word is equivalent to trusting Him! Don't just read the Word to fulfill a daily religious obligation, but instead approach it reverently, understanding that it is full of power. Receive it as if it is your daily food, because it is the food we need for our spiritual strength. Trust it to do the work in you that needs to be done. Just as we trust the medicine in a prescription to work healing in our bodies, we can trust the medicine (healing power) in God's Word to heal our souls.

I want to suggest that you consider turning what you are reading into prayers. For instance, as you read instructions about the importance of loving others, don't merely read, but ask God to help you love others. As you read about the importance of forgiving your enemies, turn it into a prayer. Ask God to always help you be quick to forgive and generous in mercy. By doing this, we are not merely reading the Word, but we are asking God to make it a reality in our lives.

Always remember that the most powerful thing we can do is lean on, rely on, depend on, and put our trust in God!

CHAPTER 20

Trusting God to Change People

Learn to value people where they are, not where you would like them to be.

John Maxwell

I think one of the easiest things in the world for humans to do is find fault with each other, but it is also one of the saddest! We all have flaws, and yet it seems that in our pursuit to change other people, we become blind to the things in ourselves that need to change.

Only God can truly and effectively change people, because change is something that must be done from the inside out. The heart must change for the behavior of a person to truly change, and only God can give us a new heart. In Ezekiel 36:26, He says, "I will give you a new heart and put a new spirit within you, and I will remove the heart of stone from your flesh and give you a heart of flesh." That basically means that God will give us His heart and Spirit, and take the hard, stony heart out of us and replace it with one that is sensitive to His will and touch. Without this change, there isn't much hope of people truly loving one another and getting along peacefully.

There may be someone in your life whom you would like to see change. It could be a spouse, child, parent, other relative, friend, or coworker. People won't change unless they want to, so the first step is to pray for them, asking God to give them a willingness to face the truth about their behavior and a desire to change. The only thing you can do after that is be a good example to them and focus on their good traits instead of the ones you don't like.

Pray with Humility

Praying for others to change must be done with all humility, or we may fall into the same trap we think others are in. 1 Corinthians 10:12 says, "Let the one who thinks he stands firm [immune to temptation, being overconfident and self-righteous], take care that he does not fall [into sin and condemnation]." I usually pray like this:

> "Father, I am asking that you change _____ if they truly need to change. If they don't, then change my heart and let me see my own error in thinking they do. I also ask that you change me in any way I need to change. Amen!"

There are many things that we know are sinful because it is made clear in God's Word, but there are lots of other things that we don't like about people for no reason other than we just don't like them. When people are not like us, or have different opinions than we do, it is easy to find fault with them, but it is wiser to broaden our circle of inclusion and learn that every person has value if we will only look for it.

One of the biggest struggles in our lives is usually with people and the things we don't like about them! We want them to change for our benefit, but we rarely consider how truly selfish that kind of attitude is—at least that's how I used to be. In our pride, we assume that our ways of being and doing are right and that all other people in the universe should do things our way. It is this very attitude that causes most divorces and the failure of multitudes of other relationships in families and life in general.

Our first step toward humility should be to realize that there is probably more wrong with us than the people we are judging. However, we don't see our faults, partly because we are so preoccupied with the faults we think we have spotted in other people. We also tend to make excuses for ourselves when our behavior is less than stellar, but we don't extend that same degree of mercy to others.

One of the greatest shocks in my life came when God introduced me to me! I was in the process one day of praying for Dave to change when God interrupted my prayer. Can you imagine that—I was trying to pray and God interrupted me! When I think back now, I am embarrassed by how foolish I was, but at the time I was totally clueless. God interrupted me while I was praying for Dave and told me that Dave wasn't the problem in our relationship—I was. I was shocked! Over the course of the next three days God confronted me with the reality of what it was like to live with me. He revealed how selfish and controlling I was, how difficult I was to get along with, and how I could only be happy when I was getting my way. I cried for most of those three days, but it was the beginning of some healthy changes in my life.

> *One of the greatest shocks in my life came when God introduced me to me!*

The Power of Mercy

Mercy always triumphs over judgment (see James 2:13). In other words, mercy is a greater thing than judgment. I doubt that any of us can show others much mercy unless we have truly realized the depth of our own frailty, weaknesses and mistakes. When we realize how much mercy God gives us each and every day, it makes us generous in giving mercy to others. Here is a cute fable about a king who did not understand mercy and a gardener who did:

A king had a large orchard. He had a variety of fruit trees planted there. He employed a skilled gardener to take care of the fruit trees.

Each day, the gardener would pick the ripe and juicy fruits from the various trees and gather them in a basket. Every morning when the royal court was in session, the gardener would give the fruits to the king.

One day, the gardener collected some cherries and took them to the king. The king was in a bad mood. When he chose a cherry to taste, it was sour. So he took out his anger on the gardener. In anger, he threw a cherry at the gardener. It hit him on the forehead, but the gardener said, "God is merciful!"

The king inquired, "You must be hurt and angry but you say, 'God is merciful.' Why?"

The gardener said, "Your Majesty, I was going to bring pineapples for you today, but I changed my mind. If you had thrown a pineapple at me, I would have been badly hurt. God was merciful for having changed my mind."

The gardener had obviously learned to trust God even when things seemed unfair. Things can always be worse than they are, and if not for the mercy of God, they would be!

We need no other reason to show mercy to others than the fact that God has and does show us mercy. And He expects us to give to others what He generously gives to us. He forgives us and expects us to forgive, He loves us unconditionally and expects us to love others in the same way, and He gives us mercy for our failures and expects us to give mercy to others. God doesn't expect us to give what we don't have, so He equips us with every good thing that we need so we might be able to enjoy our lives and represent Him well. I would imagine that the merciless king thought a long time about the merciful attitude of the gardener! When we show mercy to people, it amazes them, especially if they are fully aware that they deserve punishment.

I would like to suggest that you take a few minutes and ponder if there is anyone in your life that you need to extend mercy to. Mercy is a gift. It cannot be earned or deserved, but when it is freely given, people experience the power of God's love in a practical way that often changes them.

God gave Dave and me the grace to forgive my father for sexually abusing me as a child, and we reached out to him with mercy in his old age and took care of him until he died. I remember when he said to us, "Most people would have wanted to kill me for what I did, but you have always been kind to me!" He did receive Jesus three years before he died, and I am thankful for that. God showed him mercy through us. God works through and in partnership with people, and He wants to use all of us on a regular basis. There are multitudes of people in the world who are lost and hurting. They may have tried some brand of religion and been disappointed, but if they encounter Jesus, they will never be the same. Perhaps He can only reach someone in your life through your example. Let's be committed to showing people what Jesus is really like instead of merely trying to tell them. Words can be cheap and powerless if there is no action to back them up.

I saw lots of people over the years try to talk my father into changing his behavior because he was mean and abusive most of his life, but no matter how much anyone talked to him, it never did any good. However, when he experienced God's mercy, it began to melt his hard heart and God was able to change him. After he received Jesus as his Savior and was baptized, he truly did change. He only lived for three more years, but thankfully, he is in Heaven now.

Free Choice

God doesn't force people to do things that are against their will, and we shouldn't try to either. It isn't wrong to try to talk to someone about wrong behavior in their life that is hurting them, yourself, or others, but if they reject our words, we are wasting our time if we keep trying to convince them to change. I've seen some amazing changes in people over the years, but it was never because I was able to talk them into changing. God made the changes as we prayed!

God's Word says that if a woman has an unsaved husband, she might win him over with godly behavior, but not with her conversation (see 1 Peter 3:1). I am sure that when a woman tries to convince her husband to change, he only digs in deeper and becomes more determined not to change! God is much better at convincing people to do something, or not to do something, than any of us will ever be.

Make a commitment to pray instead of trying to change people and you will see much better results.

Presumption

The sin of presumption is one that we rarely hear about, but we need to hear more about it. Presumption comes out of a heart of pride, and someone who presumes things makes decisions that they have no authority to make and does things that they have not received permission to do.

A presumptuous employee rarely gets promoted, a presumptuous child ends up losing privileges, and a presumptuous child of God will have to be dealt with before they can be effectively used in God's work. Making our own decisions without acknowledging God is presumption.

Come now, you who say, Today or tomorrow we will go into such and such a city and spend a year there and carry on our business and make money.

Yet you do not know [the least thing] about what may happen tomorrow. What is the nature of your life? You are [really] but a wisp of vapor (a puff of smoke, a mist) that is visible for a little while and then disappears [into thin air].

You ought instead to say, If the Lord is willing, we shall live and we shall do this or that [thing].

But as it is, you boast [falsely] in your presumption and your self-conceit. All such boasting is wrong.

James 4:13–16 (AMPC)

Taking action without acknowledging God, praying and trusting Him for direction, is not something that is applauded in Heaven! It shows an attitude of pride that needs to be dealt with in our lives.

Deciding that a person needs to change and taking on the job of trying to change them is presumption. That is why I highly recommend that even when we pray for God to change someone, we do it with an attitude of humility, realizing that we also have plenty of things in ourselves that need to change.

I am glad when God is patient with me, but there have been many times when I questioned His patience with others. We don't always understand why God doesn't make a person change who is not treating us properly. According to Paul, God shows people kindness and delays judgment in order to lead them to repentance (see Romans 2:4). If God can show mercy and put up with bad behavior in an effort to bring a person to repentance, perhaps we should consider doing the same thing.

I once had an employer who did not treat his employees

properly. He wasn't appreciative of their hard work, didn't pay them properly, was quick to correct any little mistake, and wasn't very respectful. He was a Christian and should have known better, and I must admit that I often questioned God about why He was letting the man get by with his bad behavior instead of doing something to stop him. Only presumptuous people question God! A better prayer from me would have been, "God, I know You are trying to deal with _____, and I pray that he will listen to You and do what is right. He is hurting me, but I know that his behavior is hurting You even more. Thank You, Lord, for Your extreme patience with all of us."

Sadly, the man didn't change until God had to deal severely with him. As a result, his life didn't turn out the way it could have if he had listened and submitted to God. It makes me sad when I think about it, and I truly wish now that I had spent more time praying for that man instead of being upset with him and concerned about how he was treating me.

When people in your life are not living the way they should and their behavior is hurting you or other people, be sure to pray diligently for them. Pray that they will listen to God before it is too late. That kind of merciful attitude is much better than a judgmental one! Dietrich Bonhoeffer said, "By judging others we blind ourselves to our own evil, and to the grace which others are just as entitled to as we are."[11]

We will enjoy much more peace in our lives if we pray for others instead of trying to change them, and God will do what only He can do. While we are waiting for the changes to come about that we desire in life, let's be sure that we remain faithful to all that God has asked of us. Let us be pliable and moldable in His hands and invite Him to make us vessels fit for His use!

CHAPTER 21

Dealing with Doubt

Don't dig up in doubt what you planted in faith.

Elizabeth Elliott

It would be easy to trust God if doubt never came to visit us, but it does, so we must learn to deal with it. It is easy to wish for no opposition in anything, but it isn't realistic. If only there were no temptations. If only there were no fear. If only doubt didn't exist! But they do, and yet they don't have to be the problem we often allow them to be. God tells us to have faith and not to doubt, and yet He never tells us that doubt won't come for an occasional visit. The whole reason the Lord tells us not to doubt is because He knows it will come and He wants us to be ready to deal with it swiftly and accurately when it does.

I was recently doing a television program on which I was answering viewers' questions about trust. A woman sent in a question through our website about doubt. She stated that she tries to trust God, she wants to trust God, but she cannot seem to get rid of the doubt that plagues her, and she asked me what she could do.

Perhaps you have the same question; I know that I did at one time. The truth is that we cannot keep doubt from coming and trying to steal our faith and trust in God.

We can learn to doubt our doubts!

But when doubt comes, we can choose not to let it affect us. We can learn to doubt our doubts!

When God tells us not to do something, He isn't telling us that we will never be tempted to do it or never *feel* like doing it or need to resist doing it. He is actually telling us the opposite. Why tell us to "fear not" unless we are going to have an opportunity to fear? Why tell us not to come into temptation unless we are going to be tempted? Why tell us not to doubt unless we are going to have an opportunity to doubt?

Doubt will come, but we don't need to let it make us waver concerning the promises of God.

A Biblical Example

Abraham is the best example I know of when we want to study how a person in relationship with God handles doubt. Abraham had received a promise from God that he and Sarah would have a child. His situation in the natural world was impossible because they were both past their years of being able to have children. According to Scripture, Abraham had no reason at all to hope, but he hoped on in faith (see Romans 4:18).

When he considered the impotence of his own body and the barrenness of Sarah's deadened womb, Abraham still did not weaken in faith (see Romans 4:19). Unbelief and distrust did not make him waver (doubtingly question) concerning the promise of God, because he received strength by praising God (see Romans 4:20). God's promise to Abraham and Sarah came to pass, although it took quite a bit longer than they had originally thought it would.

I can only imagine how doubt tried to keep people we read about in Scripture from moving forward with God. The Bible is filled with examples of men and women who trusted God although they experienced great opposition, hardship, and at times unjust treatment. Surely doubt visited Joseph while he was imprisoned for a crime he did not commit...and Esther as she prepared to go before the king without being invited even though it was a crime punishable by death...and Paul as he traveled bringing the Gospel of Christ, only to be faced with terrible persecution, prison, beatings, hunger, and other hardships. Yet each of these people saw the faithfulness of God, and they fought the good fight of faith.

Understanding Opposition

I recently realized that being set free from something through the mercy of God doesn't always mean the disappearance of that thing. We are free from our painful past, but it may still try to visit us occasionally. We are free from fear, but it shows up at inopportune times just to see if it can once again gain entrance into our lives.

In Luke chapter 4, we see an account of Jesus being led by the Holy Spirit into the wilderness to be tempted by the devil. During the forty days He was there, He endured a variety of temptations, successfully resisting each one. Yet the Bible states that when the complete cycle of temptation was completed, the devil went away to wait for a more opportune time (see Luke 4:13). In other words, Jesus won the battle, but other battles would come. Opposition will come!

The challenges we experience test our faith in God. It is tried in the furnace of affliction, and hopefully comes out strong and imperishable. Doubt, fear, and worry are all part of the opposition. With opportunity comes opposition (see 1 Corinthians 16:9). Paul said that when he wanted to do good, evil always came (see Romans 7:21). We don't have to let it defeat our faith, but it will come!

Opposition comes in many forms, but regardless of how it

comes, its intention is to get us to give up on the hope of receiving what God has promised us.

People who oppose us:

While we are seeking to do the will of God, we may find people opposing us. The apostles had to deal with opposition from religious leaders and the Romans on a regular basis. Jesus certainly had to deal with opposition from people who rejected and despised Him. They accused Him falsely, criticized and belittled Him, but He stayed focused on doing His Father's will. At times, the people who oppose us are the ones we depended on to encourage us, and if that happens it can be particularly painful. Jesus' own brothers thought He was mad and were embarrassed to be with Him.

Circumstances that oppose us:

We are all familiar with circumstances that stand in opposition to us and make it difficult for us to complete our goals. For one month I once kept a list of things that happened in the course of everyday life that were unexpected, frustrating, and took time and energy. During that time, I was trying to finish a book manuscript, preparing for upcoming conferences, filming for television, and traveling to share the Gospel of Jesus Christ. At the end of the thirty days, I had a very long list of opposing circumstances, ranging from spilling a red vitamin drink on a white couch to falling on the stairs.

These types of things are annoying at best, but some circumstances are more serious and require even more of our attention. When something opposes us, it stands in the way of us doing what we intend to do. We can all be assured that when we attempt to wholeheartedly follow God, Satan will find a way to oppose us.

Emotions and thoughts that oppose us:

As well as the tangible things I have mentioned, we are also frequently opposed by thoughts and emotions that are intended to weaken our trust in God. Doubt is only one of them. There are also fear, anxiety, dread, hopelessness, worry, and a host of others. However, we can be encouraged to know that many of the men and women of God who have gone before us have pressed through and fulfilled the will of God, and with the grace of our Lord Jesus Christ, we can and will do the same.

We should "watch and pray" as we are instructed in God's Word to do (see Matthew 26:40–41; 1 Peter 4:7). Pay attention to the things that oppose your faith and try to prevent you from being obedient to God. Recognize them for what they are and don't let them rob you of your inheritance from God.

Concerning doubt, remember that feeling doubt doesn't mean that you don't have faith and are not trusting God. It means that Satan is bringing the temptation to stop us from trusting Him, but we can consider the source of the doubt and realize we shouldn't believe it.

For example, let's say that I heard that someone said something critical about me, but it was someone who has criticized many people and they don't really know anything about me. I would not get upset about their criticism because I would consider the source. We should do the same thing when ungodly feelings and thoughts come and tempt us to stop trusting God. Jesus told His disciples to pray that they would not come into temptation (see Luke 22:40). Temptation would come, but they had a choice about whether or not to receive it.

For me personally, it's been very helpful to understand that just because I feel fear, it doesn't mean that I am a coward, and that just because I feel doubt, it doesn't mean I no longer trust God. We cannot defeat our enemy if we don't recognize him! Doubt is a friend of fear, and both of them are our enemies!

Tuning Out Noise

Have you ever been in the presence of an irritating noise and turned on your radio or television to keep from hearing it? I stay at a condo sometimes that is normally very quiet, but once a week in the evening, a restaurant/bar down the street has a band that plays very loud music that I don't like, and it distracts me. They have some kind of portable wall that slides open so the music blasts outside as well as inside. I have learned that if I turn my television up a little bit, it drowns out the sound of the music.

I think what Abraham did when he defeated doubt and unbelief through praising God is a different example of the same thing. He heard and felt the doubt, but tuned out the noise from Satan by offering up praise.

I've heard that part of praise is telling a tale or a story about something good that God has done. Perhaps when Abraham sensed the doubt, he started asking Sarah if she remembered the time when they left their home in Haran to follow God but had no idea where He wanted them to go. God led them, step by step, and I am sure there were many stories about the goodness of God that they could recount and talk about.

Dave and I do the same thing often. We enjoy talking about the beginning days of our ministry and all the challenges we faced and how faithful God has been. When I remember those times, I find it difficult to doubt God. That doesn't mean I don't feel doubt, but I tune it out and I consider the source!

God would not have given us any instruction in His Word not

to doubt unless He knew it would come to attack our faith. Doubt is the devil's tool to keep us from doing the things that God wants us to do and having what He wants us to have.

When Jesus was on His way to heal a man's dangerously ill daughter, others kept stopping Him and asking for healing also. He stopped to help them, and on one occasion, while He was ministering to a sick person, the man's servants came, telling them not to continue their journey because the girl had died. Scripture states that Jesus heard them, but ignored them, and told the man to continue believing (see Mark 5:22–43). You see that even Jesus had to ignore reports that were intended to bring doubt. He was tempted in the same ways that we are, yet He never sinned (see Hebrews 4:15).

Never Without a Way

In *Vine's Expository Dictionary of New Testament Words*, "doubt" is partially defined as "to be without a way," or "to be without resources." We are never without a way because Jesus is the Way (see John 14:6). We may not see the way, but that is exactly when we need to trust God. Faith and trust are for the times in life when we don't know what to do or have no resources of our own. Jesus is not only the Way—He is also our Source! There is nothing any of us will ever need that He cannot provide.

People may tell you there is "no way," and the devil may whisper that there is "no way," but you can remember that "the Way" is living in you and He is with you! Will you trust Him all the way through to victory?

Forty years ago, when God called me to teach His Word, I was working forty hours a week in addition to being a wife and mother. My busy schedule left me with inadequate time to study the Bible properly in order to prepare the teachings I was being led to do at our weekly Bible study.

I felt strongly in my heart that I should take a huge step of faith and quit my job in order to spend more time studying God's Word. Dave agreed, and I left my employment and my income. Our bills were a little more each month than Dave's paycheck, and I remember how doubt and fear would attack me, telling me that God would not provide and that I had made a bad decision to give up my job.

In my heart I felt I had done the right thing, but my head kept arguing with me. I was tormented to the point of being quite miserable. Then one morning while I was walking through the house, God spoke to my heart and simply said, "You can either try to take care of yourself and live in fear and doubt, or you can trust Me to provide for you in miraculous ways." I was at a cross-roads in my faith; I needed to stop being double-minded and decide if I was going to trust God or not.

God gave me the grace to trust, and for six years we watched God provide month after month in amazing ways. During those years, my faith grew and I learned by experience that God is faithful. I still look back and remember those years, and I am glad I had them because they were used to bring me closer to God than ever before.

If you feel God is leading you to do something but as soon as you step out in faith you are attacked by doubt, don't be surprised. Your faith is being tested, and although it may be challenging, it is a good thing. The more you learn to trust God through experience, the easier it becomes to do so. You will experience His faithfulness in new ways, and each time you do, it will make you stronger.

I once heard that doubt kills more dreams than failure ever will. Don't let doubt derail your faith. Recognize it for what it is and move past it in faith!

CHAPTER 22

How Much Experience Do You Have?

Happy (blessed, fortunate, enviable) is the man who finds skillful and godly Wisdom, and the man who gets understanding [drawing it forth from God's Word and life's experiences].

Proverbs 3:13 (AMPC)

If you have ever applied for a job, one question you were probably asked by the interviewer was, "Do you have any experience?" If your answer was yes, the next question might be, "How much experience do you have?" Even though you may have a college degree in a specific field that you desire to work in, education alone doesn't always qualify us for a position. No matter how much we think we know, unless our knowledge is tested, there is no proof of how we may perform on the job.

God looks for the same thing when He desires to use us for His glory and purposes in the earth. When Moses needed help leading the Israelites, with God's direction, he gave these instructions to the people:

> Choose wise, understanding, experienced, and respected men according to your tribes, and I will make them heads over you.
>
> Deuteronomy 1:13 (AMPC)

You may notice that the list of requirements does not mention talent! A person may be naturally talented in an area, but to be a valuable asset, they also need wisdom, understanding, and experience. Moses looked for men who had some experience before putting them in leadership positions.

When we started to build the ministry God had called us to build, we also needed people to help us. While I was talking with my pastor about some of the needs, he said, "Joyce, always remember that you never truly know anyone until you see them in all kinds of situations." Why? Because nobody knows how a person will perform until character and knowledge are put to the test. We don't even know what we will do ourselves until we have the experience of going through different challenges in life.

It is easy to think or even say that we trust God, but do we actually do it when we need to? While writing this book on trusting God, I endured a certain challenge that was painful and lasted a long time. During that time, I was able to trust God to take care of it because I have had many years of experience with Him, and I have seen His faithfulness time and again.

We can read a book on trusting God, but we will need experience in order to get really good at it. As a teacher of God's Word, I try to share with people that merely hearing or reading something is only part of what is needed. We also need to "do" what we are learning, and in the doing of it, we learn as much, if not more, than we do from the knowledge we have gained through study.

Jesus Was Experienced

Hebrews 5:8–9 (AMPC) states that although Jesus was the Son of God,

He learned [active, special] obedience through what He suffered. And [His completed experience] making Him perfectly [equipped], He became the Author and Source of eternal salvation to all those who give heed and obey Him.

Even Jesus was equipped to do the job that God wanted Him to do by going through things and gaining experience. I don't know about you, but that is encouraging to me! It helps me understand that we learn as we go, so to speak. We may find it very hard as young Christians to trust God, but as the years go by and our faith is tested, we will know that God can be trusted. Knowing based on head knowledge is one degree of knowing, but knowing by experience is much deeper.

> *Knowing based on head knowledge is one degree of knowing, but knowing by experience is much deeper.*

We need education (the Word of God), but we also need revelation, and I believe that comes from times when our knowledge is put to the test and we have the experience of seeing God's goodness and faithfulness in our own personal situations.

While the apostle Paul was instructing and encouraging the Corinthians, he told them nothing would ever come against them that was too much for them to bear; God would always provide a way out, because He is faithful to His Word (see 1 Corinthians 10:13). I believe Paul was speaking from experience. He had gone through a lot of difficult things while trusting God, and time after time he saw God deliver him or give him the strength to go through it all with a victorious attitude.

Recently, during a question-and-answer session I was doing about trusting God, a woman asked, "How can I trust God when I have trusted Him in the past and He didn't come through for me?" Twenty years ago I might have had difficulty answering her, but after forty years of experience with God, I knew the answer. I said, "If you trusted God for something and didn't get it, then you were trusting Him for something you wanted that was not in His plan for you." A person of mature faith can trust God *for* something, but if they don't get it, they continue trusting God. They trust that if what they had requested was the will of God, He would have given it to them, and they understand that if what they wanted was not the will of God, they are much better off without it. They can actually learn to thank God that they did not get what they wanted! They don't merely trust God *for* things, but all the way *through* things.

Paul said this:

> But we do [strongly and earnestly] desire for each of you to show the same diligence and sincerity [all the way through] in realizing and enjoying the full assurance and development of [your] hope until the end.
>
> Hebrews 6:11 (AMPC)

Each time we put our trust in God while going through difficulty, or when we are in need, it becomes easier to do it the next time. Little by little (sometimes very little by very little) we learn to trust God, so don't be discouraged if you don't feel that you are as successful at it now as you know you need to be.

The School of Life

We are all in the school of life, and we learn more and more as we make our journey. The psalmist David spoke often about those who have experience with the Lord. He said those who have experience with God's mercy will lean on and confidently put their trust in Him (see Psalm 9:10). As we experience the goodness, kindness, mercy, unconditional love, and generosity of God, it gives us confidence that we can trust Him in any kind of situation. Even if He doesn't give us what we hoped for, we will eventually see that He does always give us the best thing for us. Just because we don't understand God's reasons for why He does things the way He does them, it doesn't mean that His ways are not right. We eventually do understand, although sometimes it takes a lifetime to do so.

People often say, "I wish I could be young again and know what I know now," but that is impossible. We only know what we know now because we have gone through the school of life.

I was not able to put life on hold and go off to Bible school when God called me to teach His Word, but I was and still am in the school of life, and I have learned many things that I could have never learned by merely going to school.

David spoke of what he called "sanctified experiences" (see Psalm 119:7). I love that thought! Some things we've experienced probably would not have been of our choosing, yet in God's infinite wisdom they become "sanctified." In other words, they are holy experiences that are used to help us truly know God and the power of His resurrection.

During the six years that God tested our faith after I quit my job and we had to totally lean on Him, I grew spiritually in amazing ways. It was not the way I would have chosen, but it was definitely the right way!

I enjoy pondering how God took care of the Israelites while they were making their journey through the wilderness and attending the school of life. He fed them manna (a supernatural food) and they had no idea where it came from or proof, except

> Sometimes the only way we will learn to do something is when we have no other choice.

for the promise of God, that it would come the next day and the next. They literally had to trust God one day at a time. Sometimes the only way we will learn to do something is when we have no other choice.

During the forty years they journeyed through the wilderness, the Israelites' clothing did not get old (see Deuteronomy 8:4). They didn't get any new ones, but what they had lasted a miraculously long time. God said that He was testing them to see if they would keep His commands or not. You see, there is no proof of trust without a test! His purpose was to promote them into much better circumstances, but first He had to teach them to be so dependent on Him that they would never forget Him after going through the things they experienced with Him (see Deuteronomy 8:2, 7, 11).

In the school of life, I have experienced the betrayal of those I thought were good friends, the rejection of family members and friends when they didn't agree with my choices for my life, misunderstandings, false accusations, persecution, and other painful events. But I have also learned the importance of forgiving those who hurt me and of refusing to be bitter and angry. I have learned integrity, excellence, peace, patience, self-control, how to choose the right friends, to keep God first in my life, to value people, and literally thousands of other life lessons. Most of them were not easy to learn because they required a test that eventually turned into experience that now allows me to trust God with greater and greater ease as the years go by.

It Does Get Easier

I believe I can say with certainty that trusting God does get easier, as does life with Him. As we choose to "put" our trust in Him instead of in other things, we learn and we grow in our ability to do so. I have watched Dave live with what I call a "holy ease" during most of the fifty-plus years we have been married. At one time it irritated me that life seemed so easy for him and so hard for me, but then I learned that life isn't easy for any of us, but we can live with a holy ease by trusting God at all times, in all things.

Dave seems to learn a bit faster than I do. I am a little hardheaded and usually have to have a few more "sanctified experiences" than he does before I finally learn. He learned early in life to cast his care on God and let God take care of him. I recall in the early years of our marriage when we experienced difficulties that he would try to tell me that my worrying and being upset weren't going to change anything, and that I should trust God. I wanted to do that, but I simply did not know how. If you are having a difficult time trusting God, I want to assure you that I know how you feel, but I know from experience that as you continue your journey, you will learn. Don't be discouraged with yourself if sometimes you seem to have very little faith; just remember that when we use our little faith, it can become great faith over time.

Jesus told the disciples, who panicked in a storm, that they had little faith (see Mark 4:40). Yet a few years later, we see these same men exercising great faith as they actively spread the Gospel of Christ in a time of intense persecution. Their little faith grew into great faith, and so can ours. They didn't learn to have great faith lying on a beach on a sunny day—they learned it in a hurricane-type storm! They failed to trust God in the storm, but eventually they learned to trust Him at all times, in all things. These men faced death daily, and yet they continued to press on, because whether in life or death, they knew that they could trust God!

When Jesus was suffering on the cross and about to draw His final breath, His last words were words of trust. He said, "Father, into Your hands I commit My Spirit!" (Luke 23:46).

I pray that we will all learn to trust God to the very last breath that we draw! Living a life of trusting God makes a life that might otherwise be miserable, enjoyable. Trust is a powerful gift that God has given us, so let's unwrap it and use it at all times, in all of our ways.

CHAPTER 23

Committing All to God

The world has yet to see what God can do through a man who is fully committed to Him.

D. L. Moody

People always seem to have things to worry about, but there are three things that we receive more prayer requests for than anything else at our ministry: prayer for people's children and loved ones, prayer for finances, and prayer for health and healing.

Worry is an enemy of trusting God, and it attempts to continually steal our faith and keep us in the realm of fear. No person ever received what they wanted from God through fear. It is only through steadfast faith and trust in God that we may live the life we truly want to live and have the peace and joy we desire. Let's look at these three areas of worry, realizing we may apply the principles we see here to any area of our lives.

1. Worrying about Our Children

How will they turn out? Are we good parents? How should we correct them when they need it? Are we too strict, or perhaps not strict enough? If we see our children struggling in areas of their lives as they grow into teenagers and young adults, we often wonder if mistakes that we made are the root of their problems. The devil loves to load parents down with false guilt that is useless and energy-draining.

Dave and I have four grown children and eleven grandchildren, and we have watched them struggle with many different varieties of personal problems. God has taught me that prayer is my greatest friend and the most potent helper I have when it comes to helping them with their struggles. My worrying about what they worry about won't help them or me.

We may see our children or others we love making bad decisions, and we desperately want to convince them to change. However, most of the time, even if we do know the answer to someone else's problem, they will not listen to us. Especially teenagers and young adults, it seems, need to make their own mistakes and find out for themselves what works in life and what doesn't.

Because Dave and I have so many grandchildren, right now we have someone in every age category, and currently we have two teenagers, who both struggle in totally different ways. One of them struggles with insecurities that manifest in many different ways, while the other one feeds anxiety in her life through constant and excessive reasoning and a sense of false responsibility.

It is easy for me at my age and with my level of experience to look at both of them and quickly locate the root of their problems, but it is not easy for them, simply because they are both still figuring life out. They are trying to understand themselves and fighting for their independence while simultaneously clinging to their sometimes childish and youthful ways.

We have other grown grandchildren whom we have watched struggle with other problems and have come through to a safe place; they are now living godly, fruitful lives. One of them struggled with anger, another with drugs, another with extreme rebellion, and I can look back and see that fervent prayer for them produced marvelous results over time. Prayer should never be viewed as a last resort, but instead it should be the first thing we do in every difficulty. Prayer opens the door for God to work, and that

> Prayer opens the door for God to work.

door is kept open as we continue to pray and thank God that He is taking care of the things and people that we have committed to Him.

Our four children each had issues, as most children do, but they are now grown men and women, all serving God, and we enjoy wonderful friendship with all of them and could not be more proud of them. You may be going through something with one of your children, or all of your children, and your concern may be based on some serious problems that definitely need God's attention. The temptation for parents is to worry. We want to help our children! We want to deliver them! We would rather take their pain upon ourselves than watch them go through things. That is how the love of God responded to our sinful condition and the misery it caused, and it is quite normal for us as parents to feel the same way. However, we cannot deliver our children from all discomfort in life, and at times we must, out of true love for them, let them suffer the consequences of the seeds they have sown. We can put confidence in the Scripture in Proverbs that teaches us to train up our children in the way they should go and when they are old they will not depart from it (see Proverbs 22:6).

Even though children may go astray for a period of time, they will be drawn back to doing what is right if we continue praying and setting a good example for them.

Whose fault is it?

If you have a child who has a problem or some measure of brokenness in their life, whose fault is it? Did you make mistakes as a parent that caused their problems, or was it just bad choices on their part? Was it the people they chose for friends or merely the society they are part of today?

I think we spend way too much time trying to place blame and not nearly enough time realizing that no matter whose fault it is, God is the answer! I definitely made mistakes with my children, yet I am actually surprised I was as good a parent as I was. I was raised in an extremely dysfunctional home, filled with one bad example after another, and yet God gave me grace to parent my children much better than I could have imagined. My two daughters have both said, "Mom, considering the way you were raised and the abuse you endured, you did a fantastic job of parenting us!"

We must remember that even if we are not perfect parents, God can overcome and fix the results of any mistakes we made. All He needs from us is a repentant heart and sincere prayer that releases the problems to Him so He can work on them.

I urge you to resist the temptation to worry about your children, and instead trust God to do in them what you cannot do. Only God can change people! I know that when I say, "Don't worry about your children," it is much easier said than done, but I can promise you that God is faithful, and although we cannot control the choices that others make, our prayers can open the door for God to work in their lives. There is no problem too great for Him.

We can commit our children to God and He will guide us in our parenting and work with them throughout their lives to keep them on the narrow path that leads to life, or we can worry about them and be fearful they will get hurt or make wrong choices. I have tried both, and I can assure you that committing them to God is by far the best choice. Our faith and trust are released through prayer and our confession. Pray for your children and say what you pray. When they make choices that appear to be in opposition to God's will, continue trusting Him. Never put a time limit on trust!

> *Never put a time limit on trust!*

We can pray for our children and others that we love and care for the same way that the apostle Paul prayed for those he loved and ministered to. Use this Scripture as an example of how to commit people to God:

> And now [brethren], I commit you to God [I deposit you in His charge, entrusting you to His protection and care]. And I commend you to the Word of His grace [to the commands and counsels and promises of His unmerited favor]. It is able to build you up and to give you [your rightful] inheritance among all God's set-apart ones (those consecrated, purified, and transformed of soul).
>
> Acts 20:32 (AMPC)

Here is an example of how to pray this Scripture and make it more personal. Let's say the person you want to pray for is named Sam, and instead of worrying about Sam and perhaps trying to change him, you have come to the place where you are willing to commit him to God. You do so with these words:

> "Father, I commit Sam to You. I deposit him in Your charge and I commend him to the Word of Your grace. I trust You to keep Sam safe and draw him into a close personal relationship with You."

Now, anytime you are tempted to worry about Sam, turn the worry into a prayer of thanksgiving that God is working in Sam's life.

I have seen amazing things happen in the lives of my children by following this method myself. At times I have prayed specific Scriptures over one or another of my children for months and have been amazed to watch God work. Worry and fear do not move the hand of God but faith, trust, and commitment do.

2. Worrying about Finances

We need money to get by in life, and it seems there is never enough of it! Once again, worrying about the problem is not the answer. God instructs us to bring tithes and offerings into the storehouse (His Kingdom work) and He will open the windows of Heaven and pour out blessings. He will also rebuke the devourer for your sake (see Malachi 3:10–11). We cannot expect to reap if we have not sown, so the first order of business is to make sure you are being faithful in your giving, and if you are, then you can have strong confidence to go before God and pray with boldness, expecting all of your needs to be met according to His riches (see Philippians 4:19). We also need to use wisdom with the finances that we do have.

God has not promised to give us all that we want, but He has promised to meet our needs. You are free to ask for anything you want, and He has promised to give us the desires of our heart (see Psalm 37:4), but those desires and wants must not be mere carnal desires that will not benefit us spiritually.

I have watched God provide for us for many years, and His level of provision has increased over the years, but I can definitely say that we had many years that were lean ones. God does not want us to be overly focused on material things, and in His wisdom, He often withholds what we want right now because He has something better in mind than simply giving us what we want. Always remember that a delay is not denial, and we should trust His timing. God may withhold what you think you want because He has something better in mind for you that you are not wise enough to ask for at the present time.

Less worry about our finances and more wisdom applied toward the proper use of them is a great need in our lives. Wisdom does now what it will be satisfied with later on in life, but our society pushes us toward mounting debt through offering us many ways to make purchases and put off paying for them until later. It is called credit, and the more of it we have, the more financial problems we are creating. When we put things on charge cards that we truly cannot afford, we are spending tomorrow's prosperity today, and when tomorrow comes, we will have nothing except sorrow.

I want to lovingly urge you to be more patient in waiting for things instead of looking for ways to get what you want right now no matter what that means for your future. Saving money to pay cash for items we want is still an option that people should consider, and yet very few do.

Peace is much more valuable than possessions! And when we have oppressive debt, it steals our peace and can cause relationship prob-

> *Peace is much more valuable than possessions!*

lems. Where there is a lack of finances, there is always stress and pressure, and that frequently turns into behavior that causes problems in our relationships. If you are already deep in debt, I don't have a quick-fix answer for you, but I can promise that if you will diligently give to God first, and begin systematically paying off your debt while disciplining yourself not to make purchases you really don't need, you will eventually be out of debt and have the joy of financial freedom.

> *In most instances our problem is not that we don't have enough money, but that we spend more money than we have!*

There are always exceptions, but in most instances our problem is not that we don't have enough money, but that we spend more money than we have! Don't be a person who feels entitled to things that you have not worked for and earned. Be patient and trust God to provide the things you want at the right time!

3. Worrying about Ourselves and Everything That Concerns Us

This is probably the number one worry in the world. We tend to worry about literally hundreds of things that concern us. We worry about our health. If we should get a bad report from a doctor, our minds can quickly become absorbed with thoughts about what is going to happen to us. Will we suffer? Will we die? Although God has provided a great deal of competent medical technology, we need to remember that Jesus is our Healer! He wants us to trust Him and follow His advice in matters concerning our health.

The older I get, the healthier I become, because I continue learning wisdom regarding how to respect the body God has graciously given me. For example, we cannot live under continual stress and expect to be healthy. When I was in my thirties, I always felt bad, but now that I am in my

> *We have the privilege of trusting God to keep us healthy, rather than merely healing us when we get sick.*

seventies, I feel great most of the time! I attribute most of the change to proper eating habits, exercise, and learning how to live with very little stress, as well as trusting Jesus to work His healing power in me at all times. We don't have to wait until we are sick to ask for healing! We have the privilege of trusting God to keep us healthy, rather than merely healing us when we get sick.

God delights in taking care of us. His Word states that He is concerned with everything that concerns us:

> The Lord will perfect that which concerns me; Your mercy and loving-kindness, O Lord, endure forever—forsake not the works of Your own hands.
>
> Psalm 138:8 (AMPC)

We are His creation, His children, and He is committed to taking care of us if we will allow Him to do so. One of my favorite verses regarding the matter of trusting God is found in 1 Peter. Please read this Scripture carefully.

> When He was reviled and insulted, He did not revile or offer insult in return; [when] He was abused and suffered, He made no threats [of vengeance]; but he trusted [Himself and everything] to Him Who judges fairly.
>
> 1 Peter 2:23 (AMPC)

This one Scripture sums up everything I wanted to say in this book. We can trust God at all times, in every way, with ourselves and with everything. Nothing that we commit to Him is outside of His control. No matter how people treated Jesus, He did not try to take care of Himself, but instead He continually trusted His Father to do that.

How much stress and unhappiness do we create in our own lives trying to make sure that we are treated properly and that no one takes advantage of us? I believe it is more than we can imagine. As we approach the end of this book, I want to ask you if you are at a place in your life where you are willing to commit yourself and everything that concerns you to Jesus. Will you release yourself to Him and be fully committed to obeying Him in all that He asks you to do as you trust Him to take care of you?

How Much Do You Have "You" on Your Mind?

We worry about who will take care of us and whether or not they will do a good job. If we should become dependent upon others, will they treat us well? We worry about what others think of us and whether or not they like us. Are we pleasing them? What is going to happen in the world and how will it affect us? Will we lose our job if the economy tanks?

"What will happen to me?" is surely the greatest fear that most of us have, but the good news is that we can release that concern today and know that God will take care of us.

Ask the Lord to help you keep yourself off your mind, because the less you think about yourself, the happier you will be. While you are trusting God to take care of you, be sure to sow good seed by helping others. Each time you help someone else in need, you are sowing seed for a harvest of God's help in your own life.

I reached a point in my own life many years ago where my unhappiness was so oppressive I was willing to see anything God wanted to show me in order to simply be happy. It's a long story, but the short version is that He showed me that I was unhappy because I was selfish. I had my mind on myself most of the time, and through my excessive efforts to try and make sure that I was taken care of, I was hindering Him from being able to do so. God wants to take care of us, but we have to commit ourselves to Him.

Commit All to God

When we commit ourselves to a person or a thing, it means we give ourselves completely. We may be committed to a person or a job. We are committed to family and friends. I am committed to the call on my life to teach God's Word. But above all other commitments, we should commit ourselves to God wholly and completely, asking for His will to be done in our lives. A complete commitment does not have an expiration date. Let me suggest that you pray a prayer daily that goes something like this:

> "Father, I commit myself anew into Your hands. I trust You to take care of me in everything and in every way. Guide me and grant me the grace to follow You always. If I get hurt, I trust You to comfort me. If I get sick, I trust You to heal me. If I have a need, I trust You to meet it. If I don't know what to do, I trust You to show me. I am Yours and You are mine and I trust You! In Jesus' name, Amen!"

How can we give anything else that concerns us to God until we give ourselves to Him? Perhaps you have become a Christian by receiving Jesus as your Savior, but have you fully committed yourself to His care and keeping? I believe this is our most urgent need!

Your best life can begin right now if you are willing to cast all of your care on Jesus and let Him take care of You!

Casting the whole of your care [all your anxieties, all your worries, all your concerns, once and for all] on Him, for He cares for you affectionately and cares about you watchfully.

1 Peter 5:7 (AMPC)

I have enjoyed writing this book and I pray not only that you enjoyed reading it, but also that it will be a book you return to often as you refresh your commitment to trusting God in all things, at all times!

NOTES

1 "Trust," Webster's Dictionary 1828—Online Edition, http://webstersdic
tionary1828.com/Dictionary/trust.

2 "Trust," Merriam-Webster.com, www.merriam-webster.com/dictionary/
trust.

3 Dr. Erwin W. Lutzer, "Who Can You Trust?," Moody Church Media, 2002,
www.moodymedia.org/articles/who-can-you-trust/.

4 "Charles Dickens Quotes," Goodreads, www.goodreads.com/quotes/188
76-no-one-is-useless-in-this-world-who-lightens-the.

5 "John Bunyan Quotes," Goodreads, www.goodreads.com/quotes/41980-you
-have-not-lived-today-until-you-have-done-something.

6 "Saint Augustine Quotes," BrainyQuote, www.brainyquote.com/quotes/
quotes/s/saintaugus108487.html.

7 Lee Strobel, "Why Does God Allow Tragedy and Suffering?," CT Pastors,
http://www.christianitytoday.com/pastors/2012/july-online-only/does
godallowtragedy.html.

8 "C. S. Lewis Quotes About Conscience," AZ Quotes, www.azquotes.com/
author/8805-C_S_Lewis/tag/conscience.

9 "Abraham Lincoln Quotes," Goodreads, www.goodreads.com/quotes/
24046-the-best-thing-about-the-future-is-that-it-comes.

10 "Charles Spurgeon Quotes," AZ Quotes, www.azquotes.com/quote/1411293.

11 "Dietrich Bonhoeffer Quotes," Goodreads, www.goodreads.com/quotes/
328974-judging-others-makes-us-blind-whereas-love-is-illuminating-by.

Do you have a real relationship with Jesus?

God loves you! He created you to be a special, unique, one-of-a-kind individual, and He has a specific purpose and plan for your life. And through a personal relationship with your Creator—God—you can discover a way of life that will truly satisfy your soul.

No matter who you are, what you've done, or where you are in your life right now, God's love and grace are greater than your sin—your mistakes. Jesus willingly gave His life so you can receive forgiveness from God and have new life in Him. He's just waiting for you to invite Him to be your Savior and Lord.

If you are ready to commit your life to Jesus and follow Him, all you have to do is ask Him to forgive your sins and give you a fresh start in the life you are meant to live. Begin by praying this prayer...

Lord Jesus, thank You for giving Your life for me and forgiving me of my sins so I can have a personal relationship with You. I am sincerely sorry for the mistakes I've made, and I know I need You to help me live right.

Your Word says in Romans 10:9, "If you declare with your mouth, 'Jesus is Lord,' and believe in your heart that God raised him from the dead, you will be saved" (NIV). I believe You are the Son of God and confess You as my Savior and Lord. Take me just as I am, and work in my heart, making me the person You want me to be. I want to live for You, Jesus, and I am so grateful that You are giving me a fresh start in my new life with You today.

I love You, Jesus!

It's so amazing to know that God loves us so much! He wants to have a deep, intimate relationship with us that grows every day as we spend time with Him in prayer and Bible study. And we want to encourage you in your new life in Christ.

Please visit joycemeyer.org/salvation to request Joyce's book *A New Way of Living*, which is our gift to you. We also have other free resources online to help you make progress in pursuing everything God has for you.

Congratulations on your fresh start in your life in Christ! We hope to hear from you soon.

JOYCE MEYER is one of the world's leading practical Bible teachers. Her daily broadcast, *Enjoying Everyday Life*, airs on hundreds of television networks and radio stations worldwide.

Joyce has written more than a hundred inspirational books. Her bestsellers include *Power Thoughts*; *The Confident Woman*; *Look Great, Feel Great*; *Starting Your Day Right*; *Ending Your Day Right*; *Approval Addiction*; *How to Hear from God*; *Beauty for Ashes*; and *Battlefield of the Mind*.

Joyce travels extensively, holding conferences throughout the year and speaking to thousands around the world.

Joyce Meyer Ministries
P.O. Box 655
Fenton, MO 63026
USA
(636) 349-0303

Joyce Meyer Ministries—Canada
P.O. Box 7700
Vancouver, BC V6B 4E2
Canada
(800) 868-1002

Joyce Meyer Ministries—Australia
Locked Bag 77
Mansfield Delivery Centre
Queensland 4122
Australia
(07) 3349 1200

Joyce Meyer Ministries—England
P.O. Box 1549
Windsor SL4 1GT
United Kingdom
01753 831102

Joyce Meyer Ministries—South Africa
P.O. Box 5
Cape Town 8000
South Africa
(27) 21-701-1056

100 Ways to Simplify Your Life
21 Ways to Finding Peace and Happiness
Any Minute
Approval Addiction
The Approval Fix
The Battle Belongs to the Lord
*Battlefield of the Mind**
Battlefield of the Mind for Kids
Battlefield of the Mind for Teens
Battlefield of the Mind Devotional
*Be Anxious for Nothing**
Being the Person God Made You to Be
Beauty for Ashes
Change Your Words, Change Your Life
The Confident Mom
The Confident Woman
The Confident Woman Devotional
Do Yourself a Favor…Forgive
Eat the Cookie…Buy the Shoes
Eight Ways to Keep the Devil Under Your Feet
Ending Your Day Right
Enjoying Where You Are on the Way to Where You Are Going
The Everyday Life Bible
Filled with the Spirit
Good Health, Good Life
Hearing from God Each Morning
*How to Hear from God**
How to Succeed at Being Yourself
I Dare You
*If Not for the Grace of God**
In Pursuit of Peace
The Joy of Believing Prayer
Knowing God Intimately
A Leader in the Making
Life in the Word
Living Beyond Your Feelings
Living Courageously
Look Great, Feel Great
Love Out Loud
The Love Revolution
Making Good Habits, Breaking Bad Habits
Making Marriage Work (previously published as *Help Me—I'm Married!*)
*Me and My Big Mouth!**
*The Mind Connection**
Never Give Up!
Never Lose Heart

Joyce Meyer Spanish Titles

*Study Guide available for this title

Books by Dave Meyer